D1498332

FLORENCE NIGHTINGALE

Nurse to the World

Lee Wyndham is the author of more than forty books. Among these are:

FLORENCE NIGHTINGALE: Nurse to the World

BALLET FOR YOU

BETH HILTON: Model

BINKIE'S BILLIONS

BONNIE

CANDY STRIPERS

GOLDEN SLIPPERS

HOLIDAY BOOK: Thanksgiving

HOW AND WHY WONDER BOOK OF BALLET

SIZZLING PAN RANCH

THE TIMID DRAGON

WRITING FOR CHILDREN AND TEEN-AGERS

FLORENCE
NIGHTINGALE, Pseud.

Jane A. L. Hyndman

Nurse to the World

LEE WYNDHAM

Illustrated by Richard Cuffari

THE WORLD PUBLISHING COMPANY

New York and Cleveland

Published by The World Publishing Company
110 East 59th Street, New York, New York 10022
Published simultaneously in Canada by
Nelson, Foster & Scott Ltd.
Manufactured at World Publishing Press, a division of
The World Publishing Company, Cleveland, Ohio
Library of Congress catalog card number: 78-82782
Designed by Jack Jaget

Contents

6

About This Book

THE NAME OF Florence Nightingale will always be associated with the profession of nursing—as we know it. But how this came to be is a story so remarkable that it should be as familiar as this great lady's name.

She was born into a family of wealth and high position. She could have spent her life as a social butterfly, for she was elegantly beautiful, well educated, accomplished, and brilliant. She had friends and admirers in England and Europe. She could have been a duchess if she had wished.

Instead, Florence Nightingale chose the lowliest of the professions of that day: nursing.

It is possible to know a great deal about Miss Nightingale —even her innermost thoughts—because from the time she was a very young girl she was in the habit of keeping diaries and writing personal notes, none of which she ever threw away.

As well as short notes and long letters to family and friends, copies of official letters and documents were also kept, and exist today—thousands of them, safely locked away in boxes in museums and private collections.

This biography of the great lady who is known as the founder of modern nursing is based on extensive research in England as well as in the United States, and the incidents dramatized in the story of this remarkable life are all based on events that actually happened or on probable happenings.

I am indebted especially to Sir Harry Verney, Bart., Miss Nightingale's grandnephew—the last person living today who actually knew this great lady—for his advice and assistance and the invaluable material lent to me. I am indebted to my brother and sister-in-law for the leg work and the copying of letters, documents, and photographs, and to Teri Martini, who helped sort these things out as well as my own mass of notes.

Special thanks are also due to the Matron and Sister Tutor of St. Thomas's Hospital and the Nightingale Training School for nurses, in London; to the Editor of *Nursing Times,* for particular information on Miss Nightingale's famous lamp; to Miss Marcia Andrews, R.N., who put me in touch with the authorities at the Harper Hospital in Detroit, on the subject of the Nightingale pledge; to these authorities at Harper; and to the kindness of the Nurses' Alumni Association of the University of Maryland University Hospital for information on the Nightingale cap "inherited" under very special circumstances by the school. And last but not least, to Lucy Ridgeley Seymer, a Nightingale Nurse herself, for information on a certain small diary kept by Florence Nightingale as a child, now alas mysteriously "lost." Perhaps this notice will help bring it back to light again.

—LEE WYNDHAM

FLORENCE NIGHTINGALE

Nurse to the World

Lea Hurst

FLORENCE NIGHTINGALE gave Granny Evans a gentle pat as she moved past the bed to the door of the dingy one-room cottage. In the short time allowed for visiting in the village today, she had tried to set the place to rights. Poor Granny Evans was nearly helpless now, spending most of her time in bed.

Opening the door a crack, Florence saw that her older sister, Parthe, was still alone in the open summer carriage under the trees of the village street. She sat there with her sketchbook, drawing the thatched cottages of Papa's tenants. Parthe never went inside a cottage. She said the closed-in smell of the rooms made her ill, but she was willing to drive down into the village with her mother and Florence now and then.

Florence glanced up and down the street between the rows of cottages. Her mother was not in sight. She must still be distributing to the tenants the jars of broths and jellies and boxes of arrowroot powder for puddings she had brought. Next time they drove down, there would be clothing and blankets and swaddlings for the new babies, simple medicines and much-needed supplies. Mama saw to it that Papa's poorest tenants had the necessary things. But Florence liked to slip in bits of ribbon and lace for the girls and young women, and toys and trifles for the children.

Now that she was older, Florence felt much more responsible for Papa's tenants and she intended to spend a great deal more time among them.

"Miss Florence . . . be ye gone?" The frail old woman called uncertainly.

Florence returned to her side at once. "No. I'm still here," she said, her voice soft and gentle. "Let's plump up that pillow. There! Now you can sit up and see the flowers I brought you. And I've some beef broth warming on the stove."

"You're a good kind miss," Granny Evans quavered. "And you've grown into a right proper young lady since the last time you been here."

"I am fourteen," Florence said gravely.

She was slim and tall, her gray eyes attentive and sympathetic. She had a smooth delicate skin and wavy bright chestnut hair that fell thickly to her shoulders. Now she moved with a natural, unhurried grace, her skirts swaying.

Granny Evans shifted her old bones on the creaking bed. "It's a wonder you keep remembering us simple folk—after you being in London and all—and only just come back to Lea Hurst for the summer," she said.

"But I love it here!" Florence exclaimed, pouring the soup into a big mug. "Each time we go away I can hardly wait to get back."

"Back here? To the likes of us?" Granny's voice rose in astonishment.

"To this very spot—and to everyone here," Flo declared. "Drink this," she added, holding the mug close to the aged lips. She stood patiently, leaning against the hard wooden bed and wondered why old Mrs. Evans would not have her window open to let in the air and sun. It was so dark and stuffy in the cottage.

"There, Miss Florence. I can't take another drop," the old woman said. "I'm that weary."

"Take a nap then," Florence suggested, easing her down in the bed. "I'll look in on you tomorrow. Your granddaughter will be here soon to look after you, won't she?"

"When she's through at the stocking mill. 'Bout supper time," the old woman replied sleepily.

Florence glanced about the bare, dreary room and wished she could do something that would really help Granny Evans, and the other people in the village too. There was so little she could do, so very little. . . .

She felt rather than saw the shadow in the doorway. It was her mother, beckoning impatiently. With a last look at Granny Evans, Florence picked up her own empty basket, her bonnet, and tiptoed away.

"Really, Flo," her mother began to scold as soon as the cottage door closed behind them. "Can you never keep track of time? Parthe and I have been waiting and waiting for you to get through in there."

Parthe had put away her sketchbook and was frowning at her sister. "I think you like sick people better than well people," she said. "I don't see why Mama—"

But Mama and Flo were in the carriage and the horse's head was turned uphill toward Lea Hurst. Whatever else Parthe was going to say was jounced out of her as they went over a rut in the dirt road. Florence fluffed her hair off her neck and immediately her mother said, "Do put your bonnet on, Flo. You must protect your complexion."

Dutifully Florence slipped on the deep straw bonnet and tied the wide ribbons firmly under her chin. Hot, tiresome things. Beside her Parthe sat, prim and proper, with every blond hair in place and her muslin dress spotless. Parthe almost never displeased Mama. Florence sighed.

"We have guests coming for dinner," Mrs. Nightingale was saying as she urged the horse up the slope. "I really should not have come down to the village today. . . ."

Florence did not hear. Her attention was elsewhere. As they drove uphill she was watching for the first breathtaking glimpse of the Nightingales' summer home, Lea Hurst. Papa had designed the house himself. It was built so high on a breezy hill that the clouds seemed to brush the steeply pitched roofs. The Derbyshire countryside rolled away from it, with lawns and terraced gardens. Three ranges of hills, blue with heather, could be seen from the windows. The view was so immense that visitors said it gave them a feeling that the whole house was floating on air.

Now Florence listened for a familiar sound above the *clop, clop* of the horse's hoofs. There it was! The rushing roar of the River Derwent that flowed between its purple banks below the house. The sound had put her to sleep ever since she was a little girl.

Both Florence Nightingale and her sister had been born in Italy, not England. Their parents had spent the first three years of their married life traveling about Europe. Parthe had been born in Naples, and a year later, on May 12, 1820, a second daughter was born in the city of Florence. Mrs. Nightingale had a fancy for unusual names, and Mr. Nightingale thought a person's name should mean something. So both girls were named after the cities of their birth. (Parthenope was the Greek name for Naples.) The girls were seldom called by their full names, however. The older sister was called Parthe or Pop; Florence's name was usually shortened to Flo.

Soon after the family returned to England, Mr. Nightingale built the mansion, Lea Hurst, on the huge estate he had inherited in Derbyshire. Mrs. Nightingale liked living here from July to October. But then Derbyshire, in the north of England, became too cold. It was also too far away from the social life she loved in London. So Mr. Nightingale bought still another house, even larger, called Embley Park, in Hampshire, where they lived for the rest of the year.

As was customary among wealthy English families in the 1800's, the Nightingales traveled from one elegant home to another—from Lea Hurst to Embley—at regular intervals, with occasional visits to the fashionable seaside, and to London.

During these journeys by carriage they drove through the nearby factory towns, and Florence could not help but shudder when she saw the squalid, crowded houses where the workers lived. And though parts of London were grand, the Nightingale carriage also rumbled through many a narrow street jammed with ugly slums. The ragged poor people and their little scarecrow children appeared even more wretched and pathetic in the murky London fog than in the countryside.

Frequently the sight caused Florence to burst into tears, and then wonder at Parthe's composure. "Don't *you* feel sorry for these unfortunate people?" Florence demanded one day as she dabbed at her own tear-filled eyes.

"Of course," Parthe replied. "But what can I do about it? Or you, Flo? Do be more sensible."

Mrs. Nightingale reached out a gloved hand and patted her younger daughter. "Your father and I do what we can for the people on our land. As for these miserable city folk—" Mrs. Nightingale shrugged her fur-caped shoulders. "It is sad to think that there must be poor and hungry people in the world. Be thankful that God has blessed *you* with a comfortable home, a mama and papa who love you, and a dear sister like Parthe."

Florence *was* thankful for her blessings. But she wished she could share them with the poor—everywhere.

It was true that Papa was generous with his farm and village tenants in Derbyshire. He and Mama even supported a school where the village children could learn to read and write and do simple sums. There too Florence helped. But it was not enough . . . not enough. . . .

Florence shook her head vigorously and realized that their summer carriage had whirled into the driveway. Her mother brought it to a smart halt before one of the side doors. She handed the reins over to Flo. "Drive on to the stable," she directed, "and then come back to the house at once. Both of you. Parthe, see to it that Flo does not linger anywhere! I must wash and change immediately, and you do the same." She disappeared inside the house with a flurry of instructions as Flo flicked the reins.

"Hurry!" Parthe said. "There's so much to do. I'm to help check the table setting and arrange the flowers for the drawing room. I wish you would learn to do that, Flo. It would please Mama." Flo was always carting flowers to the villagers, but she obstinately stuffed them any old way into Mama's beautiful vases.

"Oh, Pop," Florence moved restlessly. "All that seems so unimportant. I don't want to spend my time arranging flowers and having tea parties and dinner parties, and visits, visits, visits—back and forth endlessly. I don't see how you and Mama endure it."

"But Flo, that is what we are meant to do. That is what every well-brought-up young lady is expected to do—until she marries."

"And then?" Flo challenged. "Then it is all to do over again. Sometimes I am so bored by the visits and the visitors that I want to jump up and tell people how I really feel." Florence ignored her sister's horrified expression and went on. "I even wish we were back at Embley, having lessons with Papa."

Parthe made a face. "Not I. You know how I hate those hours and hours Papa insists we spend on our lessons. Oh, I like music and art with our governess. But all that history and Latin and Greek and philosophy and modern languages and mathematics that Papa wants us to learn! I don't see of what use that is to us—and neither does Mama."

Parthe even sounded like Mama, Florence thought. But unlike her sister, Florence enjoyed her lessons with Papa. He made all the subjects come alive. Even the difficult ones became a challenge. Florence liked using her mind, and worked hard at her lessons while Parthe made no great effort over hers and escaped to Mama as often as possible. As a result Parthe grew closer to her mother, while Flo's attachment to her father deepened.

The girls were at the stable now and a groom ran out to take charge of the horse and carriage. The sisters jumped out.

"I'll only be a moment," Flo said, turning toward the stable door. "I want to see how the pony with the swollen knee is doing."

"No you don't!" Parthe grasped her sister firmly by the hand and pulled her back toward the house. "Have you forgotten already what Mama said? No lingering! You and your pets!" she went on. "A pet pony, a pet donkey, a pet nuthatch, a pet *pig*! You try to make a pet of everything. Really, Flo!"

Mrs. Nightingale happened to glance down out of her window as the girls came into view. She saw clearly who was pulling whom and shook her head ruefully. She could always depend on Parthe—but oh, that Flo!

Flo's Secret World

FLORENCE became increasingly difficult as the years passed. Her mother blamed it on Mr. Nightingale. All those studies were giving Flo strange and unsuitable notions. She was developing a stubborn resistance to the duties of her social position. It was, of course, quite customary for the ladies of the great country houses to be concerned with the welfare of the poor. But Florence was making it practically a full-time occupation. Worse, she was actually trying to *nurse* those people.

She did have a way with the sick, Mrs. Nightingale admitted. And to keep Flo more involved in the family circle where she belonged, her mother encouraged her to help care for the various close relatives who fell ill or had babies. That was different.

"But to nurse *strangers!* How disgusting!" Parthe exclaimed. "What will people think?"

Mr. Nightingale, when he heard of Flo's village nursing, was alarmed. "She must stop it at once," he insisted. "Where does she get such peculiar ideas?"

Mrs. Nightingale was more annoyed than worried. "Do not excite yourself, my dear," she soothed her husband. "I'm convinced this is only a passing fancy with Flo. Our daughters are growing up," she continued. "Soon Florence will be going to parties and meeting young men, and that will change her outlook entirely!"

For Flo it was a difficult winter. She was sixteen and restless. The family was back at Embley Park and now Mama demanded a great deal more of her.

Mrs. Nightingale always preferred life at Embley Park. The house was so much larger than Lea Hurst, which had only fifteen bedrooms. This one could accommodate five guest families with their children and servants. And it was a comfortable distance to London and to the dozens of relatives of their closely knit family. There were scores of friends and acquaintances, too, who drove down for a day or a week or a month. Embley was constantly filled with company. Mrs. Nightingale loved to entertain. So did Parthe. Mr. Nightingale tolerated the continual commotion. Florence hated it more and more.

She grew bored with the endless rounds of tiresome gossip. Rather than play the dutiful daughter of the hostess in the drawing room, she spent her time amusing the bevies of children the guests brought with them—inventing games, play acting, telling stories, or cuddling the babies, whom she adored.

Alone in her room however, she would clasp her hands tightly and wonder, "What are any of us doing that is really important or useful?"

There was no one with whom she could share her troubled thoughts, so Florence took to writing what she called "private notes." In these and in the diaries she kept from time to time, she poured out her innermost feelings. She wrote on anything that came to hand—a scrap of paper, a blotter, the back of a calendar, old envelopes. None of these was ever thrown away.

In February, when Florence was not quite seventeen, she experienced something so strange that she did not tell anyone about it. Instead she recorded it in a private note. "On February 7th, 1837, God spoke to me and called me to His service." Flo was deeply religious and often prayed for guidance. The voice she heard was very real to her and she remembered it all her life.

After this, Florence was filled with a deep sense of peace and awareness of her own worth. She felt she had been chosen. She had a mission. She did not know what it was, but she was convinced that it would be revealed to her in time. She was content to wait.

When the family moved to Lea Hurst for the summer, Florence worked harder than ever among the poor. At the same time she was alert for any sign that might reveal what God's purpose was to be for her.

The idea of nursing as a life work did not enter her mind. Nursing simply was not done by young women in her position. The women who were called nurses were considered such low creatures that their characters could not be discussed with a young lady of Florence's tender years. Hospitals were filthy pesthouses to which the wretched poor were carted to die when there was no one to care for them. People were usually nursed at home. Doctors instructed servants or members of the family on proper care. The thought of going to a hospital was enough to give a respectable body heart failure, the villagers often assured Flo. "And your Mama would not want you even to *think* of such places."

Still, Flo was curious about hospitals. Why should they be so dreadful? There was something terribly wrong. Someday she meant to see for herself.

Before she could carry out any such plan, her mother announced that the family would go abroad to put the finishing touches to the girls' education and social accomplishments.

The Nightingales had such a splendid time abroad that they stayed on the continent for a year and a half. They attended concerts, operas, glittering social events. There were court balls where grand dukes and dashing young officers danced attendance on the charming Nightingale sisters. Both girls spoke excellent French, as well as some German and Italian. And Florence was especially well read for a young lady of that day. She collected admirers wherever she went. She looked very elegant in her Paris costumes. She was a graceful dancer and a lively dinner partner, witty and never at a loss for words.

At such times Mrs. Nightingale smiled triumphantly at Mr. Nightingale. All the bothersome nonsense had blown right out of Flo's head, just as she had said it would. Flo even outshone Parthe in the social graces. She was a brilliant success and in due time she would make a brilliant marriage. Now they must return to England. The girls were old enough to be presented at court and to be launched into British society.

The prospect of going home immediately was a shock to Florence. Suddenly she realized that her enchantment with her social life had all but drowned out the meaning of the Voice that had spoken to her two years before. She had not heard it again. Why?

The answer was quite clear to her. She was not worthy. She had been seeking idle pleasure, instead of preparing herself for her special mission. Her first duty now must be to make herself worthy of God's notice.

In March, before the Nightingales left Paris, Florence wrote a private note in which she resolved to overcome the temptation "to shine in society." The resolve was more easily made than kept. She was surrounded by opportunities "to shine"—and she was eighteen, vivid, and much sought after.

The Nightingales returned to England on April 6, 1839. Mrs. Nightingale decided that they would spend the social

season in London. They could not go to Embley because that
great house was being remodeled. It was no longer large
enough for the many guests Mrs. Nightingale planned to
entertain now that her daughters were grown up.

Once settled in a London hotel, Florence and Parthe
were caught in a whirlwind of preparations. To be presented
at court was a great social distinction and everything must be
done perfectly.

The elegant Nightingale sisters were ushered into the
glittering drawing room of Buckingham Palace on May 24,
the young Queen Victoria's own birthday. The new Queen
was surrounded by her court. When Florence's turn came to
be presented, she curtsied deeply. As she rose, her eyes met
those of the young Queen. Victoria was twenty. Only a year
older than herself, Florence thought. Yet she was ruler of
the whole of England.

The Queen's blue eyes were friendly, interested. She gave
Florence a gracious nod and a smile. The presentation was
over. Florence bowed and stepped back. She did not know
that she and the Queen were destined to meet under vastly
different circumstances.

There was a great ball after the presentation, followed by
many parties. Again Flo's "call" grew faint as she went
breathlessly from one gay party to another.

In September of 1839 the Nightingales moved back to
Embley.

It wasn't long before Mrs. Nightingale and Parthe found
Florence "difficult" again. Once more she was at work
among the villagers, feeding them medicines, making their
beds, rubbing their backs and doing goodness knows what
else. The quarreling this occasioned at home became unbearable.

There was one person in the family to whom Flo could

turn for comfort. That was Aunt Mai, her father's sister. Aunt Mai had given Florence and Parthe their first lessons. Then she married Uncle Sam Smith, Mama's brother, and went to live in a home of her own. Whenever it was allowed, she whisked Flo away for a visit.

Now Aunt Mai came to the rescue and invited Florence to London. It was during this visit that Flo decided to take up the serious study of mathematics with a tutor—a project her mother considered utterly ridiculous for a woman. But Flo's knowledge of mathematics was to serve her all her life. Now it occupied her restless mind. When she returned home, Mama and Parthe found her more agreeable, though still subject to dark moods of discontent.

"And that in spite of every social success and advantage," Mama complained to a close friend. "I cannot understand the girl. She is gay and witty in society. She could have any number of suitors. And yet she is not happy. Why?"

Had Mrs. Nightingale been closer to her daughter and more sympathetic, she might have been able to answer her own question. Florence's sensitive nature had always made her too much aware of the two kinds of life around her.

England was passing through a difficult economic period. It was the time of a great industrial revolution, a period of adjustment in which the very poor always suffer the most. Wages were low and there was much unemployment. The "hungry 1840's" brought cruel hardships to the unskilled and ignorant. It seemed to Flo that too many of her parents' wealthy friends remained untouched by the sufferings around them. Whenever a carriage whisked her to a ball or a party, to a grand dinner or concert or the opera, there was always a knot of ragged and wretched people gathered in the street, staring at the fine ladies and gentlemen who swept past them into the warmly lit, glittering interiors of the splendid buildings. Their pinched, starved faces and hopeless eyes haunted Florence. Could nothing be done for these unfortunates?

Gradually she began to meet interesting and important people at the brilliant affairs, and to discover that some of them were as concerned as she with the suffering of the poor. One was a young man named Richard Monckton Milnes. It took Florence no time at all to find out that he was not only wealthy, wise, and kind, but interested in helping young people in trouble with the law. Richard also had an endearing way of treating all his fellow men as if they were his brothers and sisters.

Florence began to see a great deal of him—and her mother could scarcely conceal her pleasure. Richard Milnes was one of the most eligible bachelors in England.

But while Mrs. Nightingale was thinking of an excellent marriage for her daughter, Florence was writing, "My mind is absorbed with the suffering of man. . . . The people I see are eaten up with care or poverty or disease." And as she read the words over, it seemed to her that her destiny, her mission, was among the unfortunate people of the world. She felt a step closer to the final revelation.

Florence's life continued as before. Then, in 1844, she could no longer keep the obvious conclusion from herself.

A Glimpse of the Way

HER LIFE work lay among the sick. In no other work did she feel so content and useful. But her work must no longer be confined to the village poor or to her family. It must be on a much larger scale. She must work in the hospitals.

Years later she wrote, "Since I was twenty-four there never was any vagueness in my plans or ideas as to what God's work was for me. . . . The thoughts and feelings that I have now I can remember since I was six years old."

And well she might. For even at the age of six she was practicing "nursing," often escaping from Mama's visitors to tend her ever-ailing doll family, or bandage the broken heads or legs of Parthe's carelessly handled dolls. She had made a tiny prescription book—no bigger than a postage stamp—for the dolls' medicines, painstakingly sewing the pages together. The medication had been solemnly recommended by an amused family doctor: "powders—16 grains for an old woman, 11 for a young woman, 7 for a child . . ." This tiny evidence of Flo's early interest is preserved in a museum to this day.

Yet because of her upbringing and the prejudices and customs of her time, it took Florence Nightingale seven long years to recognize her mission—and nine more were to pass before she was able to begin working at it.

Now, Florence knew, she would need a great deal of courage and wisdom. She could not burst in on her family and tell them about her resolve. "Hospital" was a dreadful word in 1844. She must plan to bring the subject up in exactly the right way. It was absolutely necessary for her peace of mind to have her parents' approval. It was also absolutely necessary for her to pursue this work.

What arguments could she use to plead her case? Actually, she had never been inside a hospital. And as for training to be a *nurse*—there! the terrible word was out—where could she go? There were no training schools, and she had never met anyone who had been *taught* how to nurse. The general opinion was that one needed only to be a woman, and be willing to care for the sick!

Florence had worked among the sick long enough to know that special knowledge and skills were required. How often had she stood by helplessly, unable to relieve suffering! Tenderness and sympathy were not enough. A nurse needed to know the effect of disease on the human body. She had to be aware of advances in medicine. Only then could she carry out intelligently the orders of the doctors. This idea, so obvious to Flo, was in fact revolutionary for her time, not only in England, but everywhere else in the world.

Not far from Embley there was a well-known hospital, the Salisbury Infirmary. The head physician was Dr. Fowler, an old family friend. Flo went to him with her plan to *study* nursing.

At first Dr. Fowler did not believe that Florence was serious. Then he took her through the hospital. "It won't take you long to change your mind," he said.

Entering a ward, Flo was almost overcome by the dreadful odor. Quickly she raised her handkerchief to her nostrils.

Dr. Fowler smiled ruefully. "That is what is commonly known as 'hospital smell,' Florence. It is a combination of dirt, diseased flesh, and poor sanitation. Have you had enough?"

With an effort Flo mastered her mounting nausea. "We have only begun," she said, and forced herself to look about. "Are the floors and walls never washed?"

"Oh yes, when we can get men to do it. We have the walls scraped with lime—to kill the smell. The workmen who do this often become ill themselves. It is not a popular task."

Why the men fell ill was not investigated. Germs and bacteria and their relation to infections were still mysteries to the doctors. And the use of antiseptics was still twenty years away.

"Isn't it possible to let in some fresh air? To open a window?" Florence asked.

"As you can see, the only source of heat in this ward is that single fire at the far end. In cold weather our windows must be kept closed for warmth."

Flo gazed over the crowded room. There were at least fifty beds there, standing no more than two feet apart. The sheets and blankets were filthy. Most of the patients looked miserable and neglected.

"These are the difficult conditions under which we doctors must work," Dr. Fowler said. "Now that you have seen them, surely you will change your mind about nursing."

But Florence was more determined than ever. Something had to be done to improve these horrible conditions.

"Where are the nurses?" she asked.

At that moment a coarse, dirty woman with a puffy face plodded into the ward. She bent over a patient, poked him roughly and said something to him in a hoarse, grating voice.

The color drained out of Florence's face, then flooded back in indignation. She turned toward Dr. Fowler, but he

had his arm under her elbow and was leading her away from the ward.

"That is our worst problem of all," he told her. "The women willing to work as nurses are untrained and uneducated. Some can neither read nor write. Many are always drunk. That is why they can't find jobs as kitchen maids, in far easier work and pleasanter surroundings. And some—" Dr. Fowler stopped himself and coughed delicately. "In short," he said, "it would be unthinkable for a young lady like yourself to associate with them."

Flo's gaze did not waver. "It is even more unthinkable to me that the poor and helpless sick must suffer for lack of proper care," she said quietly.

Dr. Fowler was impressed by her attitude. But he very much doubted that she would have the strength to carry through her remarkable ideas. Reluctantly he agreed to help her with her "training"—if she could get her parents' consent, of course.

In December, while Dr. Fowler and his wife were visiting the Nightingales, Florence chose the moment and made her announcement.

"Mama, Papa, you both know that I have always been interested in caring for the sick. Now Dr. Fowler has consented to supervise my training at Salisbury Hospital for a period of three months so that I can be a real nurse. With your permission," she said earnestly, "I should like to begin immediately after the holiday season."

Flo had expected her family to oppose the idea, but she had not been prepared for the stark horror in her mother's face.

Her father was speechless. Parthe began to sob. Mrs. Fowler, who had been told of Flo's plans, looked as if she wished she were somewhere else.

"Florence!" her elegant, beautiful, always proper mother

shrieked. "Do you want to disgrace yourself and your family?"

Mr. Nightingale found his voice. "Dr. Fowler, how can you have encouraged such madness?" he demanded.

There was a frightful argument. Flo had counted on Dr. Fowler to support her. But the red-faced doctor admitted that the plan presented difficulties. It must be abandoned. He would not look at Flo's stricken face.

She was bitterly disappointed, sick in heart and mind. She did not know now which way to turn. Yet she knew that what she wanted to do was right.

Although the Nightingale household was in an uproar for days, they still had social engagements to keep. Dinners and visits were the farthest things from Flo's thoughts. Yet she had to accompany her mother and Parthe on these occasions and be "witty and merry."

It was well that she did, for now came the next step in her preparation for her life's work. Flo's gift for making friends and enlisting them to her cause was already evident. She told a young lord of her interest in improving conditions in hospitals, and he listened attentively. "But I do not know enough about the subject," she confessed, "and Mama will not hear of my going near a hospital."

"Then the hospitals must come to you," the young lord said decisively. "You must study the Blue Books and hospital reports. In that way you will learn what is wrong and can consider what might be done. I shall have some sent to you at once."

The Blue Books were Government publications bound in blue paper covers—long, complicated official reports. The ones Florence received were concerned with public health, sanitation and conditions among the poor. The material required careful, thoughtful reading—and secrecy. If her mother had known what Flo was reading, she would have burned the lot.

Florence got up before dawn and worked by candlelight,

wrapped in a shawl, for she did not dare light a fire in her fireplace. She filled notebook after notebook with organized details so she could compare facts and figures. She wrote to hospitals all over England for more information. She wrote to important people she had made friends with in Germany and France during her family's tour abroad and compared the information they sent her with the situation in England. Her brilliant mind sorted and stored everything. Eventually her studies would make her a world authority on hospitals. For now this was an all-absorbing interest that eased her frustration.

When the breakfast bell rang, she put away her charts and notebooks. She smoothed her hair, brushed out her clothes, and went downstairs.

In October the Prussian ambassador sent Flo the *Year Book of the Lutheran Deaconesses of Kaiserswerth*. This told the story of the Lutheran Pastor Fliedner and how, in a little German town on the Rhine, he ran an orphanage, hospital, and school for the training of Protestant deaconesses to nurse the sick.

As she read of the work and training of these good women, Flo could scarcely contain her excitement. They were not nuns bound by sacred vows but women with a dedication to relieve suffering. *This was the place for her!* Her parents could not object to this. The religious atmosphere, the strict discipline of the nurses—everything sounded perfect.

On October 7, 1846, she wrote a private note. "There is my home, there are my brothers and sisters all at work. There my heart is and there, I trust, will one day be my body."

She treasured the *Year Book*—but she did not yet dare mention Kaiserswerth to her family. First, there was a problem she had to resolve.

A Fateful Meeting

The problem was Richard Milnes.

He had been courting Florence for years. He was sympathetic to what he knew of her dreams, for he was kind and charitable. Florence could well imagine what life would be with a fine man like Richard.

But it would not be fair to marry Richard and hope to carry through her work in hospitals as she now saw it. He would want a wife completely devoted to him, one who could happily enter into his social life, and be a mother to his children. He had every right to expect this. . . . But it would mean renouncing her mission. She could not do that. Neither could she bear to send Richard away forever.

Flo's mother became impatient, then angry. She accused her daughter of being ungrateful, of not appreciating her good fortune in having Richard's love. What on earth was she waiting for?

The strain of her own indecision and the constant nagging of her family finally brought Flo to the verge of a nervous collapse. Suddenly everyone was worried about her and a trip abroad was suggested. Selina and Charles Bracebridge, who were good friends of the family, were to spend the winter in Rome. It was decided to send Florence with them.

Selina understood Flo. Along with the visits to art galleries, palaces, and churches, she allowed Florence to visit hospitals and orphanages too, and to study the work done by Catholic sisters in these institutions. Florence did not mention these visits in her letters home, but she filled her private notebooks with the useful facts she learned.

It was in Rome that Selina introduced Florence to Liz and Sidney Herbert. It was a fateful meeting. The Herberts were a handsome couple, recently married, and Mr. Herbert was a distinguished statesman with an important position in the Government. The Herberts and Florence liked each other, and so they met frequently to go sightseeing and for other diversions.

One of the things that drew them together was Sidney Herbert's interest in building a small rest home on his estate in England. Here working people who had been discharged from hospitals could stay and regain their strength before returning to their jobs. Such a thing was almost unheard of in those days. Florence was eager to know more, to see the plans for the buildings, to learn how the place would be run and the people cared for.

When she returned to England, Florence visited the Herberts at their country estate in Wilton. There she met a number of important people who were also interested in hospital reform. When the soft-voiced Florence contributed some unexpected and accurate details to the conversations, everyone gazed at her in astonishment. How had the fashionable Miss Nightingale managed to learn so much!

Later, Liz Herbert said, "You seem to have so many facts at your fingertips, Flo."

"I do. See for yourself." Flo opened her traveling case and showed Mrs. Herbert the notes she had been collecting for over five years.

"Oh, Flo, I do so admire your determination and courage," Liz Herbert exclaimed, and she threw her arms impulsively around Florence.

Mrs. Nightingale was pleased by Flo's friendship with the wealthy and important Herberts. She had no idea, of course, that they approved of Flo's ambition to study nursing, and of her plan to go to Kaiserswerth.

While Florence was turning over in her mind the ways and means of getting to Kaiserswerth, Richard Milnes insisted on an answer. Would she or would she not marry him? He had to know definitely. Now. Florence refused him. She *had* to—for his sake as well as her own.

Mrs. Nightingale was not only disappointed. She was furious, and she let her feelings be known. Parthe wept constantly. She simply could not understand Florence. Mr. Nightingale became disgusted with all this female hysteria and took himself off to London.

Florence felt crushed, and defeated. Had she made the right decision? Had she given up Richard for a dream that would never come true? The constant quarreling at home did not help. Florence began to walk about with a blank look on her face. She was always tired, uncertain, tearful. On several occasions she fainted during family "discussions."

Selina Bracebridge sped to the rescue again. She and her husband were going to Egypt and Greece. The climate was so healthful. Would Mrs. Nightingale permit Florence to go with them?

The journey through Egypt and Greece should have been exciting, but Flo remained pale and listless. By this time Selina had learned of Kaiserswerth and what it meant to Flo. She consulted her husband and a few changes were made in their traveling plans. They would return home by way of Germany, she told Florence. She and her husband would spend two weeks in Düsseldorf—and Florence could go on to Kaiserswerth, which was only six miles away.

At first Florence could scarcely believe she would get her wish. And then she grew frightened. What would her mother and father say? But when they reached Berlin and the Bracebridges arranged for her to visit some of the German hospitals and charitable institutions, Flo forgot all her qualms. Her spirits lifted immediately.

Flo reached Kaiserswerth on July 31, 1850, and was welcomed by Pastor Fliedner and his wife. Eagerly she inspected the hospital, observed the deaconesses at work, and the condition of the children in the orphanage. Her two-week stay was all too short. "I could hardly believe I was there," she wrote in her diary.

Florence left Kaiserswerth on August 13, "feeling so brave as if nothing could vex me again," she wrote. She planned to return as soon as proper arrangements could be made to begin her training. Surely there would be no more objections at home. She was filled with love for her family, certain of their approval and understanding.

She arrived at Lea Hurst on August 21, in high spirits. There was a loving reunion with her family. But this happiness lasted only a few hours. The moment they heard of her visit to Kaiserswerth, Mrs. Nightingale became furious and Parthe again had hysterics. Florence had behaved shamefully. She was never to mention Kaiserswerth again. She would be forced to behave dutifully, to stay at home and engage in the life proper to her upbringing and station.

Within a few weeks Flo felt as broken in spirit as before. In January 1851 she wrote, "What is to become of me? . . . Why can't I be satisfied with the life that satisfies so many people? . . . What am I to do?"

In April she was able to get away from her family and visit Liz Herbert at Wilton. Immediately she felt refreshed by the Herberts' friendship, approval, and interest. And among the guests she found there was an astonishing young woman

—*Doctor* Elizabeth Blackwell. The first woman to be granted a medical degree in the United States! Now she was continuing her studies in Europe. Florence regarded Dr. Blackwell as a creature from another world. How had she ever managed to break through the ironclad traditions! The fact that she had done so strengthened Flo's sagging courage. She could not hear enough of Dr. Blackwell's experiences.

When Florence returned to Embley, she brought Dr. Elizabeth Blackwell with her. Mrs. Nightingale was startled by their guest's title, and not at all reassured by her experiences in the hospital world. Florence caught her mother watching Dr. Elizabeth as if she couldn't imagine how she had managed to remain a lady—after all *that*.

One afternoon as Florence and her guest walked about the grounds, Dr. Elizabeth turned toward the great house of Embley and remarked on how beautiful it was.

Florence stared at her home. "Do you know what I always think when I look at that row of windows? I think how I should turn it into a hospital, and just where I should place the beds."

The meeting with Elizabeth Blackwell, the glimpse of Kaiserswerth, the approval of the Bracebridges, and the encouragement of the Herberts all served to change Flo's attitude toward her family. In her diaries she argued it all out with herself. "I have been so long treated as a child and have so long allowed myself to be treated as a child. . . . Now I am thirty-one. . . . Now no more childish things, no more vain things, no more love, no more marriage. Now, Lord, let me only think of Thy will."

On June 8, 1851, she set down her decision to leave home and take up her studies. "I must expect no sympathy or help from them," she wrote. "I must *take* some things, as few as I can to enable me to live. I must *take* them, they will not be given to me."

Two weeks later she arranged to go to Kaiserswerth to study for three months.

If Mrs. Nightingale had thought Florence difficult before, she now found her impossible. No arguments, no tears, no scenes had the slightest effect on Flo's decision. Her mother finally faced the fact that her daughter was leaving—with or without her consent.

"Very well," she said. "But you will leave my way. Everything must be done in secret for the sake of your family. You can see for yourself how ill Parthe is—worrying over you. We shall say that she has been ordered to go to Carlsbad for a three-months' cure. We shall leave together, and you can go on to—to *that* place, then rejoin us and we'll come home together. You are to tell no one about it. No one."

"The Herberts know," Florence pointed out. "And the Bracebridges, and Aunt Mai."

"You are to tell no one else, then," Mrs. Nightingale insisted. "You are not to write people from that place. Do you understand, Florence?"

Mama went on and on while Parthe punctuated the tirade with sobs. Papa finally stalked out of the drawing room. He found the eternal bickering unbearable. He too was disappointed in his daughter. Mr. Nightingale refused to go with his family to Carlsbad. He shut himself up in his library, with his books.

For Florence, the trip was a painful one. There were constant complaints and arguments with her mother and sister. Even on Flo's last night in Carlsbad she was given no peace. "My sister," wrote Miss Nightingale years later, "threw my bracelets which I offered her to wear, in my face and the scene which followed was so violent that I fainted."

But Florence triumphed at last. On the following evening she reached her goal—Kaiserswerth.

Kaiserswerth

FLORENCE NIGHTINGALE'S carriage drew to a stop at Kaisers-werth and the driver helped her down. The exhausting journey from England, yesterday's bitter quarrel, a bad night's sleep, all were forgotten. Trembling with excitement, Flo watched two women in blue uniforms, with crisp white caps and aprons, approach her.

"Welcome, Miss Nightingale. Welcome back to Kaiserswerth," they said.

Flo gave the deaconesses a radiant smile. "I can't tell you how happy I am to be back," she said.

Florence had hoped to see Pastor Fliedner early the next morning and to get started on her duties immediately. But he did not summon her to his study until the afternoon. She had liked him immensely on her first visit to Kaiserswerth. But now she was no longer a guest, and the pastor seemed to regard her differently, more gravely. Flo felt that now, although he was still gracious and kind, he was passing judgment on her, weighing her character and sincerity of purpose.

She was quite right.

Miss Nightingale was different from the deaconesses he had trained, the pastor thought. They were peasant women, used to menial labor. This young woman, however, had been born into a much higher social class. She was used to a worldly, luxurious life. She had come on her first visit only to observe. This time she would have to work with those soft, delicate hands—often down on her knees. Would she resent the menial tasks? Would she last more than a week under the strict discipline at Kaiserswerth?

He said, "I am glad that you have returned to us, Miss Nightingale. You will find we lead a simple life here—but a rewarding one. I hope you will find it so."

Life was indeed simple at Kaiserswerth, but it was hard, too. Flo rose at five o'clock. Forty-five minutes later she was eating a breakfast of plain peasant food. Next, the children at the orphanage had to be fed and dressed. Then Flo went with the deaconesses to the hospital, where a hundred patients had to be cared for. How different they looked from those poor souls she remembered in Salisbury Hospital in England!

The hospital at Kaiserswerth was scrupulously clean. No patients were neglected, and most of them were even cheerful despite their illness. The sisters did their work efficiently and well, and with deep sympathy for their patients. Unlike ordinary nurses of the day, these women were good, simple people. They were dedicated to their work, and they cared for the sick with loving attention.

Soon Flo was carrying trays and helping to move patients. She washed them and combed their hair, and made their beds. Then she was taught to change dressings and give them medicines. Her hands were swift and gentle, her voice soft, her smile bright and encouraging.

"She makes me believe that I'll get well," a shadowy little woman whispered to the patient next to her.

It did not take Florence long to discover that the cleanliness and order in the hospital did not come about by chance. The deaconesses were assigned to all the tasks of cleaning—washing, dusting, scrubbing the floors.

The most difficult task Flo had ever had to do at home was that of keeping an accurate count of her mother's silver and linens. Now, when her turn came, she knelt beside the sisters and scrubbed floors as hard as any of them. She scarcely had time to eat. The sisters did not dawdle when they ate. They had only ten minutes for each meal.

Yet Florence found such new zest and happiness in this busy life, she could not bear not to share it. Her mother had said to write no one. But surely that did not mean she did not want to hear from her own daughter.

In July, 1851, Flo wrote her mother. "I find the deepest interest in everything here, and am so well in body and mind. . . . I know you will be glad to hear this, dearest Mum. . . . Until yesterday I never even had time to send my things to the wash. . . . I wish for no other world but this."

Flo soon began to feel, however, that she was not learning enough about nursing as a *profession*. All she really was doing was helping to keep patients comfortable. She was disappointed to find that there were no classes in hygiene, no real study of illness and the effects of disease on the human body. She realized sadly that the kind of schooling she wanted simply did not exist. She would have to take every opportunity to train herself.

For that matter, there was no great variety of diseases among the patients at Kaiserswerth. Only in big city hospitals could one really study disease. That would have to come later. Now she must get every bit of training available here. She decided to speak to Pastor Fliedner about an assignment to more serious duties where she could do more and observe more.

When she asked for a private interview, the pastor granted it promptly. But when she entered his study, she thought that he regarded her with disappointment. Surely this could not be because her work was unsatisfactory.

"Yes, Miss Nightingale. What is it you wish?" he asked, motioning her to be seated.

Eagerly, Flo said, "I want to learn all I can about nursing all kinds of cases. I have been present at deathbeds and at difficult births in our village and among the members of my family. Now, with your permission, I would like to observe operations and learn what I can about taking care of such patients."

"My dear Miss Nightingale!" Before she was finished, Pastor Fliedner seemed to pop up from his chair, beaming. "I had no idea—I expected—I was certain you had come to announce your intention to leave Kaiserswerth."

It was Flo who popped up from her chair now. *"Leave!* I wouldn't dream of it! My days here have been the happiest of my life. Besides—"

Pastor Fliedner finally had to hold up his hands to silence Flo's enthusiasm. "Your request is granted," he told her, smiling.

In 1851 operating methods were crude. Antiseptics—to prevent infection—were still unknown. Anesthetics—to relieve pain or put the patient to sleep—had only recently been discovered. Patients were strapped to operating tables and held by strong men. Doctors had to steel themselves against the terrible screams of the patients. Instruments used on one patient were often immediately used on the next without cleansing. Later Florence realized how dreadful this was, but at that time she accepted the practice without question.

She was near fainting at those first operations she witnessed. But she fixed her mind on the thought that whatever was being done was necessary to save the patient's life.

In letters to her mother she skipped the gruesome details, but she did mention being present at several operations, including the amputation of a workman's leg. Her mother was disgusted, her sister horrified.

In August her friends the Herberts visited Flo, and Pastor Fliedner told them that "no person had ever passed so distinguished an examination, or shown herself so thoroughly mistress of all she had to learn as Miss Nightingale."

Only one thing was lacking to make Flo completely happy —the sympathy and understanding of her family. On the thirty-first of August, 1851, she wrote a loving, beseeching letter to them, explaining once again her own feelings and her need to dedicate her life to a special kind of service.

"I should be happy here as the day is long," she wrote her mother, "if I could hope that I had your smile, your blessing, your sympathy. . . . Trust me, help me. . . . Say to me, 'Follow the dictates of that spirit within thee.' Oh my beloved people, that spirit shall never lead me to anything unworthy. . . . I cannot bear to grieve you. Give me your blessing. . . ."

It was enough to melt a heart of stone. But neither her mother nor Parthe answered Flo's anguished cry for love and approval.

Florence stayed at Kaiserswerth nearly four months. When she joined her mother and sister at Cologne, she was greeted coldly.

Parthe was as nervous and irritable as ever. "I do hope you are satisfied, Flo. I have not been able to sleep well since you left. I was simply *haunted* by the thought of the disgusting things you were doing."

"Surely now you have had enough of this mad idea of public nursing," her mother added. "Look at your hands! They are more fitting to a common drudge. You must wear gloves until they heal again, so people will not see them. When we return to England, let us have no more of these disgraceful whims of yours."

Flo pressed her lips together and said nothing. Argument was useless. For her Kaiserswerth was only a beginning. There was so much more she must learn about nursing, and she intended to learn it. There were big hospitals in London, Dublin, Paris. She would visit them all. As soon as she returned home she would begin to make the necessary arrangements. She would use the influence of her friends.

But an unhappy surprise awaited the Nightingales when they returned to Embley, and Flo had to postpone her plans. They found Mr. Nightingale resting quietly in a darkened room. Downstairs his study was closed. For weeks he had not been able to read or write.

"I'm afraid I am losing my sight," he told his wife and daughters.

"What do the doctors say?" Mrs. Nightingale fluttered

around him helplessly. "Surely something can be done. We will find someone who can help you." Her husband had never been ill before and she was terrified.

"We can go back to Carlsbad," suggested Parthe. "The mineral waters there are supposed to do wonders. You will be well there in no time."

Mr. Nightingale sighed and shook his head. It was clear he had almost given up hope.

Flo examined her father's inflamed eyes. He was obviously suffering much pain.

"Have the doctors advised you? Didn't you see an oculist?" she asked gently.

Mr. Nightingale admitted that he had. "He wants me to go to Umberslade. I must take the cold-water treatments there, he says."

"Why haven't you gone, Papa?" Flo cried.

"I don't want to go, Flo. Not unless you will come with me. I don't want any other nurse."

"But of course Flo will go with you," Mrs. Nightingale put in quickly. "It will be a fine opportunity for her to devote some of her nursing skill to her own family. Who has a better right to it?"

She gave her daughter an angry look. Flo sighed. Even at a time like this Mama could not forget her bitterness over Flo's stay at Kaiserswerth. Would her mother never understand?

Florence knelt beside her father's chair. "I'll gladly go with you, Papa," she assured him. "Please do not worry. I shall be at your side whenever you need me."

Florence and her father left for Umberslade within the week. There Mr. Nightingale's sight improved gradually. Florence read to him, walked with him, talked with him. The closeness she had once felt with her father returned. At last she felt free to confide in him.

"I do not want to hurt you or Mama. But I cannot live

the life you have planned for me. I must do what I feel is right for me," she told him.

"And what you feel right for you is to go out among the wretched poor as a nurse?" he asked her gently.

Florence nodded.

"Oh my dear, what a hard life you have chosen! I cannot bear to think of it."

"Please, Papa. It is what I want, what I *must* do. Help me! As long as I live at home, Mama and Parthe will try to stop me. You have heard the arguments. It makes us all miserable. I must be free."

Flo told her father what had happened at Carlsbad and on her trip home, and of her happiness in the work at Kaiserswerth.

Papa said nothing, but he held Florence close for a moment and kissed the top of her head. Florence's mother and sister had treated her badly. For the first time he seemed fully aware of his younger daughter's wretchedness. He must find a way to help her. She had suffered enough.

"Leave me now, Florence," he told her tenderly. "I must give this matter some thought."

When Mr. Nightingale finally came to a decision, everyone was surprised. His wife was furious, but there was nothing she could do about it. Mr. Nightingale had arranged for Florence to have an income of her own. With this money she could now live away from home, if she wished.

Florence began to make plans at once. In April, 1853, she arranged to go as a student to the hospital managed by the Sisters of Charity in Paris. She was actually packing her bags when a letter from Liz Herbert caused her to alter her plans.

The Lady Superintendent

FLO READ and reread Liz Herbert's letter with mounting excitement. "I have heard of a suitable position for you," Liz wrote. "It will require all your talents for nursing, organization and diplomacy. . . ."

The opening was in a small private nursing home—not an ordinary hospital—called The Institution for the Care of Sick Gentlewomen in Distressed Circumstances. Here ladies with little or no money, and no relatives or friends to look after them, were cared for. Many of them were governesses or paid companions, which was the only kind of work considered respectable enough for a lady who needed to earn her living.

It was unthinkable for such people to be forced to go into the dreadful London hospitals. So this project became a favorite charity of prominent society ladies. But it had gotten into difficulties because of poor management.

Now it was planned to move the Institution from its present location and to reorganize it completely. Liz Herbert had heard the news from her friend Lady Canning, who as chairman of the committee was responsible for finding a

47

superintendent to manage the Institution. Liz had at once recommended Florence in glowing terms. Florence would hear directly from Lady Canning in a few days.

Florence could scarcely wait for those few days to pass.

When the letter from Lady Canning arrived, she was thrilled with the position it described. An interview was arranged at once.

Lady Canning was a regal woman and behaved in a very formal manner. Florence could not tell whether Lady Canning approved of her or not.

"What we need, Miss Nightingale, is a capable person who can supervise the alterations of our new home. Afterward she would have the responsibility of running the entire Institution." Lady Canning paused and looked at Florence critically. "I hope you will forgive me for saying so, but you seem rather young for such a post. We had in mind a more mature person."

Flo smiled graciously—and, she hoped, confidently. But she was anxious. How much she could do in a position like this! If only they would accept her. She did her best to impress Lady Canning with her vast knowledge of hospital organization. But her youthfulness could not be talked away. It simply wasn't "proper" for a position of this kind. Was she to be denied this chance to put into practice all that she had learned? As if she were so young that she needed a chaperon. Of course! There was the solution.

"Suppose I bring with me a superior, elderly, highly respectable person—as matron or housekeeper," Flo suggested. "Would that be agreeable to the committee?"

Lady Canning looked doubtful. "I am afraid the committee would not care to add wages for such a person to its other expenses."

Flo was relieved. At least this would not be a problem.

"I would be happy to hire the housekeeper and pay her wages myself," she offered.

Lady Canning seemed pleased with this arrangement. She promised Flo an answer within the week. The committee must be consulted.

Flo was kept waiting several weeks. Then there were more interviews, with the full committee of ladies, and more questions.

"Would it be proper for a lady like Miss Nightingale to nurse women of a lower class?"

"Was it proper for a lady to be present at medical examinations?"

Like Parthe and her mother, many of the committee ladies were shocked to learn that Flo had already been present at such examinations and had actually observed operations.

Over the years Florence had learned self-control. Now her quiet, sensible manner, her obvious store of knowledge, and her personal charm and tact finally triumphed. By the end of April, 1853, the position was hers.

She was to work without pay, as befitted her social station. The expenses of the matron would be met by her also. However, she was to have complete control and management of the Institution and all its funds. Florence was quite satisfied with this arrangement.

Her duties would not begin until the new building was found, and this would be a matter of several weeks. Not one to waste time, Florence decided to resume her journey to Paris and her intended studies with the Sisters of Charity.

Her mother and Parthe had their usual hysterics. A hospital was still a hospital, even if it was called a nursing home. Florence was disgracing them again. Since Mama could do nothing about Flo's "going into service," she could see no reason for her daughter's jaunt to Paris to study at *another* hospital. Surely she could spend these last few weeks in the company of her mother and sister.

This Florence would not do.

She went abroad armed with a special permit to visit any

hospitals she chose. And, before reporting for her training with the sisters, she spent some time in inspection tours and interviews. She had many opportunities to talk to famous Paris doctors and surgeons, and to watch them at work in their clinics.

When she finally did report to the Sisters of Charity, all went well for two weeks—and then Florence came down with the measles! That was the end of her "training" in any hospital as a student. She never again had time for this kind of study. All that she knew and was to put into practice to save lives and to ease pain she learned from reading, observation, and her own actual experience in dealing with the sick entrusted to her care.

After recovering from the measles, Florence was able to return to London in mid-July. She refused to join her family at their hotel and instead took rooms of her own. During the month that followed, she had Aunt Mai's help in supervising the alterations of the new house chosen for the institution. Mrs. Nightingale would not give her blessing to the undertaking. Florence had known better than to ask.

What magnificent plans she had!

"We shall want hot water piped to every floor," she told the committee.

"Think of the expense!" cried Lady Canning. "The nurses can very well fetch the water from one floor to another."

Flo remained firm. "Nurses who have to run about fetching hot water become merely pairs of legs. A nurse should not have to leave her floor or her patients while on duty."

The committee gave its approval. Pipes were to be installed as Flo directed.

This was only the beginning. Lady Canning's committee was soon examining "windlass installations"—small, boxlike dumbwaiters—in various buildings in the city.

"Food and supplies can be lifted from floor to floor by this rope-and-pulley device," Flo explained. "This will save the nurses time and work."

These small and very handy "elevators" were installed. But there seemed to be no end to Miss Nightingale's unusual demands.

"Each patient should be able to ring for the nurse," she said. "Bells should ring in the passage outside the nurse's door. But they should be a special kind of bell. Each bell should have a valve—a little hinged lid—that will fly open and stay open."

"Whatever for?" asked the ladies. "Isn't one ordinary bell enough to summon the nurse?"

"An ordinary bell would not tell the nurse which patient has rung," Flo explained. "If the valve remains open, she can give prompt attention to the woman who needs it."

It did seem logical. And so the new bells were also installed.

Although there was some grumbling in the committee about Miss Nightingale's strange new ideas, many were pleased. Theirs would be an up-to-date institution, a model of its kind.

In August, Florence decided to move with her matron, Mrs. Clarke, into the new home of the Institution, at No. 1 Harley Street. Then she could be certain that all her orders were carried out.

During her very first week there, Flo and the committee had a serious argument. Lady Canning and several others arrived early one morning. Florence met them in her private sitting room. As they stormed in, Lady Canning waved the list of prospective patients in front of Florence.

"What is the meaning of this, Miss Nightingale?" she demanded angrily. "Here!" She pointed to a name on the list and glared at Florence.

Florence answered calmly. "It is the name of one of our new patients. Surely you do not expect me to consult the committee each time a new patient applies for admission."

"That is not the point," interrupted one of the ladies. "This woman is not a member of the Church of England! She is a Roman Catholic. We have never accepted anyone in the Institution who was not of our faith."

"You will have to send her somewhere else," Lady Canning said firmly.

Flo's gray eyes glowed with anger. Did the ladies really imagine that only gentlewomen of their own faith were worthy of medical aid? How cruel and narrow-minded. For a moment she could not trust herself to speak. When she did, her voice was icy.

"Very well, if that is what you wish. I will send her somewhere else. But then I must wish you good morning. I will begin packing my things at once. If the Institution means to turn away sick and helpless women on the basis of religion, I too must leave."

Regardless of how much she wanted this position, Florence refused to be a party to such prejudice.

The ladies were taken by surprise. The Institution was to open in a few days. Where could they find such a competent director? Miss Nightingale could not leave now! Florence was unmoved. Either the Institution was to be open to all who were in need, or she would leave. The ladies looked at one another helplessly. They needed Florence— and so they agreed to her terms.

By autumn the Institution was filled with patients. The lady superintendent seemed to be everywhere at once, managing nurses—the best decent women she could find—assisting at operations, and often nursing difficult patients herself.

Her devotion to her duties, to the smallest detail, was felt through the hospital. If the coal cellar needed checking for waste, Florence went down and checked. Cupboards and storerooms were turned out and examined with the aid of

Mrs. Clarke. Lists of things they had, and longer lists of things they needed, received her full attention.

At one point Florence discovered that the ladies on the committee had bought a small quantity of very expensive jam. But they had neglected to order the brushes and brooms and dusters she had requested. After that Flo attended to the ordering herself. As for the jam, she had her kitchen staff make it—at a fraction of the cost of buying it. The committee ladies were tremendously impressed by the saving.

Because Florence was on her feet a good part of the day and night, she wrote to Embley, asking her mother for a pair of comfortable old boots. And, since the committee had by now spent all their money, Florence appealed to her family for linen, carpets, curtains, and food for the patients.

Mrs. Nightingale still did not approve of her daughter's life, nor the joy she seemed to be taking in it. But she was becoming resigned. She began to respond to Florence's requests. Odd pieces of linen were sewn together. Old curtains were made into bedcovers. Florence's patients were provided with clean sheets and patched rugs as well as good food.

Hampers of flowers, fruit, vegetables, and meat began to arrive for the patients every week.

Parthe came around more slowly. After some coaxing, she agreed to have tea with Florence in her sitting room at Harley Street. But then, as she entered the Institution, she had hysterics and collapsed.

In spite of the problems which inevitably arose in her work, Florence was still able to write, in January, 1854, "I have never repented nor looked back, not for one moment. And I begin the New Year with more true feeling of a happy New Year than I ever had in my life."

The ladies on the committee were pleased with the work Miss Nightingale was doing. Even those who had been opposed to her ideas were singing her praises six months later.

Flo's superb gift for organization and the diplomacy with which she handled people won them over. Flo could be sweet, womanly, and gentle, but she could also be icily firm—and she knew exactly when and on whom to use which tactics.

Her patients adored her. She was never too busy to listen to their problems and their secret fears. Many times she helped her "gentlewomen in distressed circumstances" even after they had left the Institution. One of the patients was a governess who had been ill for many weeks. When it was time for her to leave the Institution, she was still weak. Flo learned that she intended to take a position immediately.

Flo shook her head in disapproval. "You are not well enough to work. You must rest or you will be back here within a month," she warned.

The woman looked helplessly at Flo. "I must work, Miss Nightingale. I have no money. I cannot afford a rest."

Immediately Florence arranged to send the governess to the country at her own expense.

When she was completely well, the governess wrote Flo a long and grateful letter. "I cannot thank you enough for this extra rest, my dear, dear Miss Nightingale. I cannot even express how much indebted I am to you."

Flo received many such letters from poor and friendless women whom she helped.

Florence's father was now a county official, and one of his responsibilities was the management of hospitals and asylums. He and Florence wrote each other frequently, and Mr. Nightingale followed Flo's work with great interest and pride.

Sometimes he was intensely sympathetic with her ordeals. At other times he was amused by the manner in which she got her way with the committee. And now and then he was even awed by the huge savings that she managed on the purchase of drugs and food for her patients.

He was the one she wrote to when things went wrong—when the heavy chimney of a gas stove came down and "would certainly have killed a patient" if Florence had not been there to catch it in her arms. Or when a drug was sent with a wrong label. The patient would have been poisoned, "if I had not smelt it before it was given to her," Flo wrote him.

Although Florence was often worried and depressed by her patients' problems, her friends did not know it. Through the years she had learned to mask her feelings. She remained a cheerful companion and a charming guest. Her popularity never waned, and bright, frivolous invitations were frequently delivered by hand to her Harley Street apartment. One said, "Lock up your ladies, leave someone else to stir the gruel, and cab round to me." And when she could, Florence did just that.

Mrs. Nightingale had been certain that the life her daughter had chosen would be frowned upon by London society, but she was wrong. Many people admired the work she was doing, and Flo was invited everywhere. She felt especially close to Liz Herbert, who had suggested her for this position. The Herberts were just as interested in hospital reform as was Florence. And Sidney Herbert was in a position to do something about it, for he had a great deal of influence in the Government.

When Florence had been the director of the Institution for almost a year, things were running so smoothly that she was becoming restless. There must be more she could do. There was something in her which never allowed her to feel that she was doing enough.

And then, in May, Liz Herbert wrote to say that Sidney wanted information about hospital nurses, their poor pay and worse lodging. If he had enough material, he might be able to get some of the evils remedied.

Flo set about gathering this material immediately.

The facts were as disturbing as ever. The years had brought no improvements in the London hospitals. The nurses still "slept in wooden cages on the landing places outside the doors of the wards . . . where it was impossible for the Night Nurse taking her rest in the day to sleep at all, owing to the noise, where there was no light or air."

Under such conditions, how could hospitals hope to get decent women to serve as nurses?

Each nurse was expected to care for a large number of patients. In one case, Miss Nightingale discovered a single nurse in charge of four wards—well over two hundred patients. As for the care given the sick, the patients came in filthy from the London slums and remained that way. "The nurses as a general rule did not wash patients." The beds smelled even worse than the poor wretches in them. Their meals were greasy messes. Even water was not taken around, unless the nurse happened to remember to do so.

A doctor in a large London hospital told Florence that there were only two nurses whom the surgeons could trust to give medicine to their patients. And a head nurse of another large institution said that "in the course of her large experience she had never known a nurse who was not drunken."

Of course the "nice" people—the ladies and the gentlemen—knew that hospitals for common folk were not *quite* what they should be. As for the nurses, "Surely they weren't as bad as all *that*," one of the titled ladies was reported as saying. "And if they do drink a little . . . poor people, it must be so tiresome sitting up all night." But just where could a better type of nurse be found? And that seemed to be that.

When Liz Herbert called at Harley Street to discuss this problem, Florence told her friend, "The 'nurses' are considered a necessary horror. If that is the way people feel, the situation will never improve."

Flo held up a letter from a doctor she had met in Paris. "This poor man asks me to recommend two reliable, skillful nurses to act as matrons. Alas, I know of no such marvels."

Liz frowned. "But there must be a way to produce such nurses, Flo. The more people hear about good nurses, the more they will want them. *You* could train such nurses. Think how well you have done with those you selected for the nursing home."

Florence shook her head. "I searched high and low for good, clean women, like my own dear Nanny Gale. And you know how difficult it was to persuade them to come to us." She sighed. "No. Student nurses should be young women. From the farms and villages, perhaps—and you know what *their* people would say about that! And even if I could get them, where and how would I train them? Certainly the Institution cannot provide money for such a project."

After Liz Herbert left, Flo paced her Harley Street sitting room, deep in thought. Something had to be done. And then, what she *could* do flashed into her mind.

The Call Is Clear

FLORENCE sought out Dr. Bowman. He was surgeon for the Institution and one of the best-known medical men of his day.

Without wasting a moment of his time, she told him exactly what she wanted—an opportunity to train nurses on a large scale.

Dr. Bowman was quite familiar with the way Miss Nightingale managed to get what she wanted. His eyes twinkled. "And of course," he said, "knowing that I hold a senior appointment on the staff of King's College Hospital, you want me to use my influence to make such training possible."

Miss Nightingale did not even blush. "Yes," she told him frankly. "Since King's College Hospital is being rebuilt and reorganized, why not have the new professional nurse come from there?"

"Why not, indeed?" Dr. Bowman mused. If someone else had proposed such an idea, he would have said that person was mad. But Miss Nightingale was an extraordinary young woman. And judging by what she had accomplished at this nursing home. . . .

"As Superintendent of Nurses I could select and thoroughly

train the kind of women we need." Florence broke gently into his thoughts.

Dr. Bowman would not allow himself to be carried away by her enthusiasm. "Do you never consider the possibility of failure?" he asked her. "The type of woman you want in your training program will be hard to find. Families of young women from good homes would discourage them from entering what is now a disreputable profession."

"Given a chance, we could change the whole outlook on nursing," Florence told him confidently.

Dr. Bowman smiled. "Very well, Miss Nightingale. I shall see what can be done."

Several of the doctors at King's College Hospital knew of Miss Nightingale's work at Harley Street. They were just as impressed as Dr. Bowman was with her special combination of talents.

"By all means, let us appoint her our Superintendent of Nurses," one of these gentlemen said at a meeting of the board of directors.

"She certainly cannot make things any worse," a less enthusiastic supporter of her cause chimed in.

In August, while these discussions were going on, an epidemic of cholera struck London.

Cholera, in 1854, was a fearful disease. It came suddenly, bringing on high fevers and terrible stomach pains. If a victim survived he was weak and ill for days; many more died than lived. The disease spread quickly through the slum districts where food and water were contaminated.

Wagonload after wagonload of frightened, hysterical patients were brought into the already overcrowded London hospitals. There was confusion everywhere. Many of the nurses caught the disease; many died of it. Others, terrified of infection, ran away.

Florence volunteered to superintend the nursing at Middlesex Hospital, but she ended up working harder than any of the ward nurses. From the Friday afternoon when she reported at the hospital till Sunday, no one saw her off her feet. She undressed, bathed, and treated the terror-stricken and pain-racked patients, comforting them as best she could. It did not matter to her whether they were respectable wives and mothers from the poorest section of town, or wretched women of the streets. Each received the same gentle handling, tender care, and attention.

When the worst of the epidemic was over, she went to Lea Hurst to rest. There, a tearful Mrs. Nightingale told a house guest, "I do not understand Flo and her terrible work at all. We only wanted her to have every advantage—a good and comfortable life. We are ducks who have hatched a wild swan."

But it was no swan that they had hatched. As a famous writer put it years later, it was an eagle. And Flo's courage and determination were soon to be known throughout the world.

The troubled, dependent daughter was gone. In her place stood an elegant, composed, independent woman. Florence's heart and soul were absorbed in her work, in her hospital reorganization plans and her schemes for training nurses.

If only there were some way to prove quickly what trained women could do to help suffering, sick persons! How much it would mean to the sufferers—and to the women themselves. It would not be an easy life, but it would be a satisfying, useful one. And it would offer an honorable occupation for women who must earn their living, as well as those, like herself, who were not content with social and domestic duties. As Flo worked among her "distressed gentlewomen," she could see no way to overcome the difficulties and the prejudices around her.

But even then, three thousand miles away, events were taking place which would offer to Florence Nightingale the opportunity to fulfill her dream.

Three thousand miles from No. 1 Harley Street, something was happening that was destined to affect the whole British Empire—and to change Florence Nightingale's life forever.

The British people depended on their vast world trade for their national wealth. For years England had controlled the entrance and the exit to the Mediterranean Sea with a navy that was unquestionably the best in the world. Now England's power was threatened by Russia, whose Tsar schemed to get control of the all-important passageway from the Black Sea. If the Tsar's navy could accomplish this, then Russia would become a first-class naval power.

This idea did not suit either England or France. Therefore, when Russians began to move into Turkish towns that lay on the shores of the Black Sea, England and France declared war. They planned not only to help Turkey win back these towns, but also to destroy the new Russian naval base at Sevastopol on the Crimean Peninsula.

To the British people, this seemed an easy thing to do. After all, hadn't they defeated the mighty Napoleon at Waterloo? But that had been in 1815, nearly forty years before. Now, in 1854, the British army was not prepared for war. National pride, however, would admit no such thing, despite the advice of some of the wiser heads in government. Even Queen Victoria and Prince Albert doubted the wisdom of this war. Nevertheless, men were drafted, equipment and supplies were hastily collected, and the troops were gaily cheered as they sailed away, their colorful uniforms blazing bravely in the sun.

It was a delightful time of year for a long sea voyage. The weeks spent aboard the troop ships in sailing around France, Spain, Portugal, through the Strait of Gibraltar into the Mediterranean were pleasant. Then more weeks passed as they steamed past Italy and Greece, through the Aegean Sea, through the Dardanelles, into the blue Sea of Marmara, the Bosporus Strait, into the Black Sea. Men who had never been far from home were entranced by the sights and sounds of the ports where the ships put in for coal, water, and provisions.

An army base was set up in Scutari. This was a Turkish village on the Asian side of the Bosporus. It lay directly across from Constantinople (now called Istanbul). The Turkish Government had turned over to its British ally a huge old artillery barracks and the General Hospital that went with it.

Some of the men were left at Scutari. Most of the army sailed on to Varna, a city on the Black Sea in Bulgaria. From Varna they were supposed to make a swift and deadly thrust at Sevastopol, the Russians' naval base in the Crimea.

But when the transports arrived to move the army from Varna to the Crimea, it was found that there were not enough ships to take both men and equipment across the Black Sea. A fateful decision was then made, one that was to have disastrous consequences. It was decided to leave the general supplies which the army usually took, and instead to cram the men, ammunition, and cavalry horses into the ships.

On the fourteenth of September, thirty thousand men landed at a cove with the ominous name of Calamita Bay, thirty miles north of Sevastopol.

The staff surgeon was aghast. "They have sent out an army without any kind of hospital supplies," he exclaimed. "There are no litters or carts or pack animals. There is nothing to work with—when the time comes."

A few days later, cholera broke out and spread rapidly. Without supplies nothing could be done for the men and over a thousand were shipped back to Scutari.

Six days later, the British and the French fought the Russians at the Battle of Alma, and won. It was a victory of sheer gallantry and courage, for the allied armies faced a withering fire from the Russian artillery.

Back in England, the people were overjoyed at the news of victory. Then the casualty lists began to come in. No battle is won without a price paid in dead and wounded. But the people at home did not know all the horror their soldiers had to face. The wounded were worse off than the dead. Because the supplies had been left in Varna, there were no bandages, no splints for broken, shattered bones, no anesthetics. There were no medicines. The soldiers lay on bare ground or on dirty straw in farmyards, for bedding too had been left in Varna.

Amputations were performed under the most filthy and brutal conditions. There were no lamps, or even candles. At night surgeons had to work by moonlight.

Then another thousand men with cholera were shipped back to Scutari. One might have thought *they* were the lucky ones. But it took from eight days to three weeks for these poor souls to reach Scutari. And when they did—

The General Hospital at Scutari might have been adequate under ordinary circumstances. But the first thousand cases of cholera had filled every bed. Now the senior medical officer, Dr. Menzies, was notified that hundreds of those wounded at Alma would be arriving shortly. The old barracks would have to be converted into a military hospital at once.

But how? The filthy old barracks was enormous. How to get it cleaned? Where to get equipment for it? Dr. Menzies was still wrestling with this problem when the wounded began to arrive. They came in terrible condition. Ships meant to carry two hundred and fifty patients were jammed with more than twelve hundred. Soldiers with every kind of wound were crammed together, and all the way to Scutari they were thrown about cruelly by the rough seas.

When they arrived, there were no beds to receive them, or nurses to care for them. They lay on the floor of the Barrack "Hospital," wrapped in blankets soaked with their blood. There was no food for them because there was no hospital kitchen. There was no water—no one to carry it and nothing to carry it in. The doctors worked heroically against terrible odds.

Scenes of horror accompany every battle. But unless one is actually there, or is told vividly what is taking place, it is impossible to imagine. Soldiers who come home do not want to shock their families. Or they want to forget their experiences. Or their memories become mercifully dulled. The British people might never have known of the horrors at Scutari if a war correspondent had not happened to be on the scene.

This man was William Howard Russell, of *The Times* (London)—and he was the very first newspaper man to report from a battlefront. Today the war correspondent is a respected figure. In 1854, when Russell's name was mentioned, one of the generals said, "I'd as soon see the devil."

The officers took no notice of him, but Russell noticed

everything. And when he sent his reports back to London to *The Times,* they were filled with fury and disgust.

His dispatches were published on October 9, 12, and 13— and the whole nation reeled with shock.

"It is with feelings of surprise and anger," Russell wrote, "that the public will learn that no sufficient preparations have been made for the care of the wounded. Not only are there not sufficient surgeons . . . there is not even linen to make bandages. . . .

"There is no preparation for the commonest surgical operations! Not only are the men kept, in some cases, for a week without the hand of a medical man coming near their wounds, but now it is found that the commonest appliances of a sick ward are wanting, and that the men must die through the medical staff of the British Army having forgotten that old rags are necessary for the dressing of wounds. . . ."

A bomb bursting on Buckingham Palace could not have stunned the British more. Before they could recover from this blast, Russell sent another:

"The manner in which the sick and wounded are treated is worthy of savages. . . . There are no dressers or nurses to carry out surgeons' directions, and to attend on the sick between visits. Here the French are greatly our superiors. Their medical arrangements are extremely good, their surgeons more numerous and they have also the help of the Sisters of Charity . . . these devoted women are excellent nurses."

This last stung the public into even greater fury against the Government. Indignant readers wrote to *The Times.* On October 14 a letter asked:

"Why have we no Sisters of Charity? There are numbers of able-bodied and tender-hearted English women who would joyfully go out to devote themselves to nursing the sick and wounded, if they could be organized for that purpose, and placed under proper protection."

While some asked questions, or wept with pity, or seethed

with rage, or wrung their hands helplessly, Florence Nightingale was taking action. On Saturday October 14, five days
after the first dispatch appeared in *The Times*, she wrote Liz
Herbert:

"A small private expedition of nurses has been organized
for Scutari and I have been asked to command it." She would
pay her own expenses and those of one nurse, she told Liz.
A contribution of two hundred pounds had been given for the
expenses of three other nurses. These nurses would pay for
their own lodgings and food and would be no expense whatever to the country. Florence had already seen Dr. Andrew
Smith of the Army Medical Board, and he had given them
authority to go.

"I do not mean that I believe *The Times* entirely, but I
do believe we may be of use to the poor wounded," Flo added
tactfully. The administration of the British Army was then
divided between two ministers, the Secretary *for* War and
the Secretary *at* War. Because Sidney Herbert was now
Secretary *at* War and responsible for the financial administration of the army, he was the target of many complaints.
Florence did not want Liz to think that she was one of
Sidney's critics.

She then asked Liz Herbert to communicate with the committee and arrange for Flo's release from duty at the Harley
Street nursing home. And did Liz think that Sidney would
approve of the plan? Would he give them any advice or
letters of recommendation? And were there any supplies for
the hospital that he would advise them to take to Scutari?

Strangely—or perhaps not strangely at all—Flo's letter
crossed one written to her by Sidney Herbert on Sunday
October 15.

"You will have seen in the papers," he wrote, "that there
is a great deficiency of nurses at the hospital at Scutari. The
other deficiencies, namely of medical men, lint, sheets, etc.,

have been remedied ere this. . . . As to medical stores, they
have been sent out in profusion. . . .

"But the deficiency of female nurses is undoubted, none
but male nurses having been admitted to military hospitals.
. . . It would be impossible to carry about a large staff of
female nurses with the army in the field. But at Scutari no
military reason exists against their introduction. . . .

"I have received numbers of offers from ladies to go out,
but they are ladies who have no conception of what a hospital is, nor of the nature of its duties. They would, when the
time came, either recoil from the work or be entirely useless, and consequently—what is worse—entirely in the way.
Nor would these ladies probably ever understand the necessity, especially in a military hospital, of strict obedience to
rule. . . .

"There is but one person in England that I know of who
would be capable of organizing and superintending such a
scheme—and I have been several times on the point of asking
you to direct it. . . . Would you listen to the request to go
and superintend the whole thing?"

Sidney Herbert then assured her that she would have
complete authority over the nurses and the fullest assistance
from the medical staff. Also she would have unlimited power
to draw on the Government for whatever she thought necessary for the success of her mission.

He pointed out the difficulties and the problems of such an
undertaking, then added, "Your personal qualities, your
knowledge and your power of administration, and your rank
and position in society give you advantages in such a work
which no other person possesses.

"If this succeeds, an enormous amount of good will be
done now, and a prejudice will have been broken. . . . I know
you will come to a wise decision. God grant it may be in
accordance with my hopes!"

It was a miracle. An unheard-of opportunity. Florence could never have hoped for anything like this. The letter trembled in her hands as she read and reread it.

At about the same time, Sidney Herbert, with equal astonishment and vast relief, was reading Flo's letter.

Before she had time to reply he was already on the way to Harley Street.

"There is more to this mission than relieving the sufferings of our soldiers," he told her as Flo led him into her sitting room. "The whole nation will be watching you. Bringing female nurses into an army hospital could be a calamity."

"Or a great victory," Flo said steadily.

"Yes," Mr. Herbert agreed. "If the nurses perform their duties well—if they prove that they are reliable, *no one will ever look down upon nurses again.*"

Had Flo needed any more convincing, this last argument would have done it. To raise nursing to the level of a respected profession for women had been her dream for years.

"It will not be easy to select the nurses you'll want to take with you," Sidney Herbert continued. "No one knows this better than you. I believe you should engage a group of forty."

Flo gasped. "Forty! I doubt I shall be able to control more than twenty."

The Secretary at War smiled. "If you were anyone else, I too would have my doubts."

When Sidney Herbert left, Flo sat alone in her room for some time. Since the age of seventeen, she had felt that there was some very special work she had to do. Now she knew what it was. Her "call" was clear at last.

Ever practical, Flo turned her attention to the immediate need. *Forty nurses!* Wherever was she to find them?

The Eagle Takes Wing

EVERYTHING moved swiftly now. Four days later, on Thursday, October 19, Florence was notified of her official appointment by the Government as "Superintendent of the Female Nursing Establishment of the English General Hospitals in Turkey."

At once the whole country buzzed with excitement. Never before had a woman been so honored. When word reached Embley, Flo's family was as surprised as everyone else. This time there were no hysterics. Suddenly Mrs. Nightingale and Parthe were enormously proud of Flo. They hurried to see her in London.

Parthe, writing to a favorite cousin, said, "It is a great and noble work . . . and one cannot but believe she was intended for it. None of her previous life has been wasted . . . her experience . . . the gathered stores of so many years . . ." Parthe burbled on for pages.

With her authority assured, Florence was determined to waste no time in getting to Scutari. After Sidney Herbert's visit on October 15, she set Saturday October 21 as her sailing date. Her good friends Selina and Charles Bracebridge had already volunteered to go with her and help her in every way they could. And Flo was pleasantly surprised and touched when her Harley Street matron, Mrs. Clarke, insisted that she was going too.

Charles Bracebridge took charge of the finances of the expedition and rushed about London making arrangements for the journey. There were only six days to sailing time!

Meanwhile, Sidney Herbert offered his London house as headquarters for the expedition. There a group of ladies, including Selina Bracebridge, Lady Canning, and Mary Stanley, prepared to receive the women who applied as nurses. Despite the high-sounding readiness which English women had expressed to go to the ends of the earth to nurse their soldiers, only those of the humblest class showed up. And not many of them, either.

Florence Nightingale was able to select only fourteen elderly women who had hospital experience. No young women were accepted, for the camp at Scutari was not an orderly place. Florence had decided that her nurses would wear plain uniforms, with no ribbons or other fripperies. These uniforms would identify her nurses and serve as their protection among the rough soldiers. *Moreover, each nurse was required to sign a pledge of absolute obedience to Miss Nightingale's orders.*

The uniforms were not attractive, but they were warm and practical, consisting of a gray tweed dress and a gray worsted jacket. Across the chest the nurses were to wear a band, embroidered in red with the words *Scutari Hospital*. A plain white cap, a bonnet, and a short woolen cloak completed the costume. Small white collars and large white aprons would be worn on duty in and around the hospital.

Florence completed her nursing staff by enlisting twenty-four nuns and sisters from religious orders. She insisted on selecting these women "with a view to fitness and without any reference to religious creed."

These nuns and sisters were not required to wear any uniforms other than the habits of their religious orders.

It scarcely seemed possible, but by October 21, 1854, Miss Nightingale and her "Birds," as the newspapers nicknamed her little band, were ready to leave.

As a last duty, Miss Nightingale called again on Dr. Andrew Smith, of the Army Medical Board, for possible advice. The doctor was in excellent humor. No doubt, he told Miss Nightingale, they would be a great comfort to the men. The ladies' finer instincts would discover such things as spots on a sheet, which male orderlies might overlook. And of course they could always give a nice soothing drink to the poor fellows who seemed uncomfortable.

Miss Nightingale managed to control herself. She said that she was thinking of taking out some needed supplies. The doctor all but laughed at that, assuring her that there was ample quantity of *everything* in Scutari—"a positive profusion of medical comforts."

After listening to his jokes, Florence Nightingale decided to follow her own instincts, and added a few more items to her already lengthy lists.

Florence took with her the fewest possible personal possessions. Among these was a small black pocket notebook in which she had tucked three letters. One of these was from her mother—the kind of lettter she had longed for, but never received till now. At long last Mrs. Nightingale blessed her daughter and her work. Another letter was from Bishop Manning, whose aid Florence had sought in enlisting the Catholic sisters as nurses. The third letter was from Richard Monckton Milnes.

"My Dear Friend," he wrote, "I hear you are going to the East. I am happy it is so for the good you will do there, and hope you may find some satisfaction in it yourself. . . . You can undertake *that,* when you could not undertake me. God bless you, dear Friend, wherever you go."

On October 21, 1854, Florence Nightingale and her group of nurses left London. They crossed the English Channel to Boulogne, in France, where they were enthusiastically greeted, especially by the French fisherwives. They knew who she was and where she was going, and many of them had sons, husbands, and brothers in the war.

The group continued on to Paris, and then to Marseilles, where they were to take ship. Florence spent several days in Marseilles purchasing large quantities of supplies. And when Flo and her "Birds" went aboard the mailboat *Vectis* on October 27, a mound of bales and boxes sailed with them.

The *Vectis* was a clumsy old paddle-wheeler, and on the second day out she ran into a fierce storm. Miss Nightingale was not a good sailor and had to take to her bed. The ship rolled, pitched, and shuddered as the seas pounded her. Parts of the ship, the steward's cabin and the ship's galley, were washed away, but fortunately none of the crew or passengers was lost.

Somehow the wretched ship survived the raging weather, and on Saturday November 4 she sailed up the Bosporus and dropped anchor.

This harbor was known as the Golden Horn, and the city of Constantinople curled around it on one side. The houses on the hills, the spires and minarets above the rounded domes of the mosques looked like a smudged watercolor in the drenching rain. Florence, who had managed to stagger up on deck, gazed at the scene briefly then turned to look at the opposite shore.

There sprawled the village of Scutari, with the huge, square Barrack Hospital set on a hill above it. Each side of the building was a quarter of a mile long, with a massive tower

at each of the four corners. The General Hospital, in which they were also to serve, stood a quarter of a mile beyond.

The nurses and nuns lined the railing. Impulsively one of them exclaimed, "Oh, Miss Nightingale, when we land, don't let there be any delays! Let us get straight to nursing the poor fellows!"

Florence shook her head. "More likely the strongest will be wanted at the washtub." She sensed the disappointment around her and her hands tightened on the ship's rail. Her nurses must be made to realize that there was nothing romantic about the work they had come to do. It would be hard and bitter and heartbreaking. Only the strongest in spirit would stand up to it. She turned abruptly and went back to her cabin.

Soon the British Ambassador at Constantinople, Lord Stratford, sent the Secretary of the Embassy to see Miss Nightingale.

The secretary delivered a flowery welcome from the ambassador, then informed her that she and her nurses were to go to Scutari at once. The Battle of Balaclava had been fought on October 25 and the wounded were expected to arrive soon.

Then brightly painted gondola-like boats, called caiques, appeared at the side of the *Vectis*. Miss Nightingale and her nurses, with their carpetbags and umbrellas, were lowered into them. As the Turkish boatmen rowed them across the white-capped bay, the caiques bobbed and dipped alarmingly. The rain had stopped and the shore could be seen more clearly, with its rickety dock and the steep slopes above it. There was no sign of a paved road, and as Flo was helped to the dock, she wondered about the wounded. How on earth did they get them up to the hospital?

Florence and Mr. and Mrs. Bracebridge led the procession toward the huge main entrance of the hospital. Their messenger-interpreter followed, and the nurses trailed behind.

The Barrack Hospital, looming above them, looked so forbidding that Selina Bracebridge reached out and gripped Flo's hand. The closer they got, the worse everything looked. There was garbage and litter everywhere, and in the building dozens of broken windows gaped to the winds.

Perhaps it was not so bad inside, Flo told herself. After all, Mr. Herbert and Dr. Smith had assured her that all necessities had been sent here.

Dr. Menzies, the senior medical officer, and Major Sillery, the military commandant, met them at the gate. They said the proper words of greeting. They asked polite questions about their journey. But Florence could find no trace of genuine warmth in either man. Well, she had not expected to be received with open arms. She and her nurses would have to prove themselves.

Major Sillery appeared nervous. "Of course you'll want to get settled," he said. "We have assigned you the northwest tower. It has a number of rooms and you will have more privacy there. If you will follow me . . ."

The women picked their way through the muddy, littered square enclosed by the barracks. Florence noted that one side of the huge building had been gutted by fire and stood unused.

As they led the way, Dr. Menzies was silent, controlling his anger. The last thing he wanted in this hospital was a pack of women to pamper the soldiers. As for this youngish society lady—at best, she might turn out to be a well-bred nuisance. At worst, she might well be a Government spy. And Dr. Menzies had something to fear on that account.

He remembered his interview with the ambassador at Constantinople, Lord Stratford. The ambassador had received a letter from the Government questioning the conditions at the Barrack Hospital. The ambassador had told Dr. Menzies that if there were shortages, as reported, there were also large sums of public money available for anything needed. After those dreadful articles by that man Russell, donations had poured in to the Government. *The Times* also had a special fund to be used for anything at all that was needed.

Dr. Menzies was horrified. His superior officer, Dr. Hall, had already sent an "all's well" report to England. If he consented now to use public funds, Dr. Menzies would be admitting that everything had been bungled. Instead he told the ambassador that all present needs were taken care of. As for the future, there were the supplies at Varna. Nothing was needed. Nothing.

Lord Stratford did not press the matter. He was more interested in his social life in Constantinople than in the hospital for common soldiers. He had readily accepted Dr. Menzies' assurances and chose to ignore the troublemaking reporter from *The Times*. The ambassador never made a personal inspection, nor did he send anyone from his staff to do so. Instead he wrote Mr. Herbert that all was well, and there was a "profusion of supplies."

Now here was Miss Nightingale—an intimate friend of the Secretary at War. Just what was the woman after? Much as he would have liked to send her packing, Dr. Menzies didn't dare. After all, she had powerful friends at home.

The group climbed a steep flight of steps. Major Sillery threw open the door leading into the tower. "Six rooms. All yours," he said.

The rooms were dark, damp, and filthy. Florence could see no furniture, except for a few chairs. There were no tables, no beds. No stoves to cook on or give off heat. Around the walls of some of the rooms ran raised wooden platforms. The Turks called these "divans," and used them to hold their bedding. But there was no bedding visible anywhere. The more Flo looked the worse it all appeared—and, she suspected, not by accident, but by design.

Major Sillery coughed apologetically. "You must understand that we can provide little in the way of accommodations, Miss Nightingale. Our first concern is for our men."

Florence smiled. "But that is as it should be," she said evenly.

The major's color heightened. He appealed to Dr. Menzies. "The doctor will tell you that we are all terribly crowded here."

"Yes, yes," agreed the doctor. "We are overcrowded already and more casualties are expected tomorrow."

Major Sillery nodded vigorously. "So you see, we have little room to spare."

"This will do very well." Miss Nightingale inclined her small, elegant head. "Thank you."

The doctor and the major excused themselves. The door closed behind them—and Selina exploded.

"Flo, this will never do! Never! Six rooms for more than forty people!"

But already Florence was thinking constructively. "One of these 'rooms' is a storeroom. We'll make a kitchen of it." She was already planning ahead. "And one a closet—I'd say ten feet square. The sixth room must be upstairs."

"We can't possibly manage in this space," Selina insisted. "What can they be thinking?"

"They can be thinking that if we are uncomfortable enough we will go home on the next boat. That is exactly what they want. It is not what I intend to do," Flo answered calmly.

Charles Bracebridge stomped about furiously. "But this is disgraceful. I'll speak with the major myself."

Flo stopped him. "I think it would not do any good. He must do what he is told—and Dr. Menzies' mind is clearly made up about us."

Tired and disappointed, the nurses began to murmur among themselves.

Florence took charge at once. "For the time being at least, we will have to make the best of things," she told them. "Now then, we'll put fourteen nurses in this large room and ten in the next. Selina, you and I will take the closet. Charles and our messenger can have the small room . . ."

The nuns were assigned the sixth room upstairs, and obediently they picked up their carpetbags and trudged up the stairs. A moment later shrieks were heard, and the eight nuns clattered down the stairs.

Flo's Battle at Scutari

PALE AND SHAKEN, one of the nuns cried, "Miss Nightingale, the room upstairs is occupied—"

Flo frowned. "Surely, sister, if you explained who you were—"

The nun shook her head. "The man is dead. He looks like a Russian general."

"Really, this is too much!" Charles Bracebridge exclaimed. He stormed out of their quarters, followed by the interpreter. They came back with two Turkish orderlies who removed the body.

If Miss Nightingale wondered how and why a dead general—a prisoner of war—had just happened to be overlooked in a tower assigned to her, she said nothing.

"What we all need," said Selina, "is a nice hot cup of tea."

It sounded so much like home that Flo laughed and it broke the tension. She felt her strength returning. "I'll go down to the kitchen and see what can be found. Why don't you all start to unpack?" she suggested.

"We'll need brooms and scrubbing brushes," Sister Mar-

garet declared. Mrs. Roberts, one of the nurses, looked
puzzled. "I don't seem to be able to find the bedding anywhere," she said.

Florence set off with a long list of the things they needed.
An hour later she returned with forty tin basins and a large
pot of milkless tea. It was all she could find. They drank it
huddled together, while Florence reported what she had seen.

"I'm afraid that nothing we read in *The Times* could have
prepared us for the actual conditions here. There is no
furniture and no equipment in this place. The men are
lying out there on the bare floor, row upon row, shivering
with cold. They have no shirts and no bedding. In one ward,
an operation was being performed before the eyes of all the
other wounded men. They did not even have an operating
table."

The nurses were shocked into silence.

"The kitchen is impossible," Flo continued. "They seem
to use thirteen huge Turkish copper pots to cook everything
—for all those men. There are no baking ovens, no proper
utensils. And there seems to be only the one kitchen."

"Thank goodness you thought to bring some supplies and
utensils for us," exclaimed Selina. "Our stores should come
in off the *Vectis* in a day or so. But the poor men!"

Florence silenced her friend with a gesture. Such out-
bursts accomplished nothing. She had already resolved to
waste no energy in futile anger, reproaches, or vain hopes.
Every ounce of strength she had would be used to forward
the success of her mission.

"For the present," she continued calmly, "the tin basins
you are holding are going to have to do triple duty. They'll be
used for washing, eating, and drinking tea."

The nurses stared at their basins, scarcely able to believe
what they were hearing.

"Er—ah, Flo," Charles Bracebridge announced reluctantly.

"There seems to be a shortage of water, too. The young chap outside tells me there is a fountain in the corridor. We are to be rationed one pint each day."

"For everything?" Mrs. Clarke sounded scandalized.

"For washing and drinking and tea," Mr. Bracebridge said heavily.

That night they all went to bed in the dark, for they had been given neither lamps nor candles. Somehow they managed without bedding, lying on the hard wooden divans or the hard dirty floor.

"At least we are all well." One of the Catholic sisters spoke out of the darkness. And all the others knew that she was thinking of the much greater suffering of the wounded in the halls beyond.

Flo lay awake beside Selina Bracebridge, staring into the darkness of their stuffy closet. All the knowledge she had acquired about nursing would be needed now. But would Dr. Menzies and Major Sillery allow her to use her knowledge?

"*Flo!*" Selina's urgent tone startled her.

"What's wrong?" Flo raised herself and peered at her friend.

"Do you hear what I hear?"

Both women sat silent, listening. There was the sound of tiny, scurrying feet and high-pitched, eerie squeaks.

Flo sighed. They might have expected this too. "Rats, Selina, rats! We'll have to do what we can in the morning. Try to get some sleep now."

"*Sleep!*" echoed Selina. "Oh, Flo!"

Somehow they did sleep. In the morning they lined up at the fountain to get their ration of water. When they returned to their quarters, they found several pails of food that had been left for them in the large central room of the tower.

Mrs. Clarke bent over to inspect it and pronounced it "Slop!" However, they all were so hungry that they closed their eyes, ignored the smell, and ate what they could.

By this time Florence had decided to station twenty-eight nurses for duty in the Barrack Hospital, and ten in the General Hospital that stood a quarter of a mile away. But the one rule she must abide by at all costs was that no nurse was to enter a ward without the request of the doctor in charge. Her appointment specifically stated that she was to work under the orders and direction of the chief army medical officer—Dr. Menzies. She waited all day, but no orders came from Dr. Menzies.

"Perhaps that is because it is Sunday," one of the disappointed nurses remarked.

Flo exchanged a swift glance with Charles Bracebridge and immediately suggested that they go to the hospital chapel to hear the sermon. If the doctors did not choose to use her nurses, she would have to keep them occupied in other ways.

Happily, their supplies from the *Vectis* began to arrive. Flo had the boxes opened and set some of her nurses to sorting the old linen that would be used for soft dressings. Provisions had to be counted, sorted, and listed. Flo intended to keep track of every item when it came and where it went. Too many supplies intended for the soldiers had vanished without a trace. She would be able to account for every single item, and for every penny spent from the money entrusted to her.

As she worked among her nurses, Flo kept her ears tuned for sounds of unusual movement outside their tower. The wounded from the disastrous Battle of Balaclava were expected to arrive today. Surely then she and her nurses would be called.

These would be the brave survivors of one of the most terrible battles of the Crimean War. The gallant light-cavalry brigade had been almost wiped out there. They had followed confused orders and charged straight into massed Russian cannon. Whatever "victory" was won had come through the sheer courage of the common foot soldiers. These were the men Florence now hoped to nurse—if the doctors would set aside their prejudices against women in army hospitals. So far, she had received none of the cooperation promised to her back in England.

"Flo." Charles Bracebridge appeared at her side. "They're landing the poor fellows now. It's horrible."

After days on a rough sea, the wounded were lowered from the hospital ship into boats. For most of the men this was torture. They were bumped and tossed over to the dock where careless Turkish orderlies hauled them onto stretchers. Their pitiful cries went unheeded. Inside the Barrack Hospital, where they had hoped for some comfort, they were dumped heedlessly on the bare floor. There were so many that most were left untended. It was like *The Times* account all over again.

From the windows of their quarters, the nurses watched the horrible scenes on the slopes. Florence hurried to Dr. Menzies and offered the services of her nurses.

"We could bathe the wounded and bring them water," she said. "Some of us would be willing to help carry stretchers. The men are suffering so."

Dr. Menzies eyed her coldly. "The British soldier is not a namby-pamby schoolboy, Miss Nightingale. You do not give the men credit for their extraordinary physical courage. Your nurses," he added, "would only embarrass them. They would be in the way."

Without another word, Florence returned to her quarters. She would not offer to send her nurses into the wards again. If she insisted, Dr. Menzies would consider it a threat to his authority. He might never forgive her. Then she and her nurses could give up all hope of becoming a useful part of the hospital. They would have to wait—no matter how difficult that waiting was—until they were *asked* to help in the wards.

The nurses did not understand this. They knew only that they had come to help the British soldiers. They wanted to rush outside and do whatever they could for the suffering soldiers. When Florence refused to permit this, they became angry.

"It's inhuman, that's what it is," one of them muttered. "How can we stand by and watch them die without doing anything?"

For a moment Florence thought she had lost control and they would disobey her orders. If that happened, all that she hoped to accomplish would be defeated then and there.

She stood before them, commanding them, willing them to

obey her. She did not raise her voice and her manner remained calm. "You must understand," she told them, "that we are something entirely new to the British Army. We must not behave like undisciplined hysterical females. If we do, the authorities will send us home in disgrace. We *can* help the wounded men—even here, in our tower."

For the next several days she kept them rolling bandages, folding soft dressings, making stump rests for the amputees, and slings for broken legs and arms. Mrs. Bracebridge and Mrs. Clarke sorted provisions and stacked them in the storeroom. Mr. Bracebridge and the interpreter went down to the village and rounded up odd pieces of furniture and bedding for the tower.

Meanwhile, Florence continued her inspection of the hospital. Somehow she must find a way for her nurses to be useful outside the tower. It must be a way that would meet with Dr. Menzies' approval.

Down in the hospital kitchen she found an attendant on duty who was willing to talk. Stepping back from a huge steaming kettle, he wiped his damp forehead with a grubby rag.

"I tell you, miss, it's a great burden, this job. We prepare three different kinds of meals here, you know. There's full rations—that is the soldiers' regular diet." He turned to a table, picked up some chunks of meat tied together with a piece of torn uniform, and dropped the bundle into the copper kettle. Several other chunks were held together with red string. These he dropped in also.

Florence tried to keep the horror from showing in her face. She made her voice even as she said, "May I ask why the meat is tied up in that way?"

The man looked surprised at her ignorance. "Why, Miss, that's for telling what belongs to what orderly. How else would we know unless the meat was tied up different?"

When he saw that Miss Nightingale still did not understand, he went on. "Look here, each orderly takes care of so many soldiers. He gets their rations himself with a signed paper from the doctor. We cook it for them here all together. But how are we to know who gets what amount of meat? So we mark it like this, with rope or a nail or a hook for the joints. Then each orderly claims what is his."

Florence watched as he began to ladle a stew—if it could be called that—from another copper pot into pails lined up beside it.

"Some men get full rations and some get only half. But a lot of 'em are on spoon diet now, poor chaps. There's lots of stomach ailments here. It's up to the orderly to give the food out according to doctor's instructions. We do everything by the book here, miss. No signed paper, no food," he finished proudly.

The smoke from the green wood fires made her eyes smart, but Florence continued her questions.

"What about extras like milk pudding or jelly? Surely those on liquid diet need more than—" she stared at the muddy water in which the meat had cooked, "than this soup?"

The man shrugged. "Oh, miss, we've no place to make extras even if we could get them."

Florence thanked him for explaining things to her and went immediately to find Dr. Menzies. It was no wonder the wounded often died of illnesses other than their wounds. The terrible food and filthy conditions would make healthy men sick.

She found Dr. Menzies at last, busy in one of the wards. Whatever might be said about him, he was a tireless doctor. He worked as quickly and efficiently as possible, but there were always more men arriving than he could handle. When Florence reached him, he looked exhausted, too exhausted to argue.

She plunged right in. "Dr. Menzies, I know you do not

approve of having my female nurses working in the wards. But we could help by supervising the cooking of special diets for the men. Your kitchen is overburdened and we would not interfere there, of course. We will make our own arrangements. Won't you let us provide the men with arrowroot and port wine? At least these will help to lessen their hunger pangs. Many have not eaten properly in weeks. . . ." She paused and wondered whether she had gone too far.

A frown began to gather on Dr. Menzies' forehead, and Flo said quickly, "We will observe all the usual rules and will never act without signed orders from the doctors. Please let us help."

Dr. Menzies gazed at her wearily. There was so much to do—so many men to attend to. Now *she* was bothering him again. Perhaps if he let her fuss with diets it would keep her so busy that she would leave him alone.

"Very well!" he snapped. "See to it, if you like. But mind you," he warned, "the proper forms must be filled out. You are to do nothing without permission."

Florence nodded and sped away. She knew that the army was simply mad about proper procedures and correct forms. It was bogged down with paper work, signing and counter-signing everything. She would go right along with the rules, now that she had a foothold. Here was something her nurses could do for the men directly.

The storeroom in the nurses' quarters soon became an "extra diet" kitchen, with Mrs. Clarke presiding over its precious stores. Florence had bought portable stoves as well as quantities of arrowroot powder. Mixed with boiling water, this swelled into a kind of starchy jelly easily digested by the sick. Wine served to warm and brace the weakened men. Beef extracts, rice, and sago-thickened puddings were useful in restoring a little of their strength.

So it was that the survivors of Balaclava were fed proper

soft invalid foods from clean pails carried by Florence Nightingale's nurses. But the nurses were instructed to do nothing, *absolutely nothing* else.

With the tower kitchen running smoothly, Florence began to plan another one. At this time there were nearly two thousand sick and wounded in the Barrack Hospital wards. Florence thought of putting a second kitchen at the opposite end of the building.

On Thursday November ninth, as she hurried past the wards to inspect the site, she came upon Dr. Menzies addressing a group from his medical staff.

"Half an hour!" exclaimed one of the doctors in response to something the Chief said. "How can we possibly get ready to receive five hundred men on a half-hour's notice!"

Dr. Menzies' shoulders sagged. His face was ashen. "I don't know. Some oversight in notifying us. . . . These are the poor devils from Inkerman. . . ."

Florence's heart lurched. The dreadful battle of Inkerman had been fought on November fifth, and now five hundred of the wounded were coming when there was scarcely enough room for the men already here!

"We must do what we can," Dr. Menzies was saying. "Round up everybody who can help. We must use every pair of hands we can find. *Miss Nightingale!*" he roared suddenly. "Where are your nurses?"

The other doctors turned to her. Their prejudices were suddenly forgotten. Miss Nightingale represented forty pairs of hands! At a time as desperate as this, desperate measures must be taken—even if it meant using civilian females as nurses in a British Army hospital!

In the face of such an overwhelming emergency, a lesser spirit would have collapsed. Not Florence. Even as she sped back to the tower to alert her people, she was already putting first things first.

The men must be bedded somewhere. Since there was little room left in the wards, the great cold halls would have to be used. There were no beds, no mattresses. But there was a stable of cavalry horses in the hospital and tons of straw for them.

Flo sent Charles Bracebridge and the interpreter to round up some orderlies to find any kind of material that could be stitched up into large sacks. Then she set her nurses to stuffing the sacks with straw.

"Between one and nine o'clock we had the mattresses stuffed, sewn up, laid down—alas! only upon matting on the floor—the men washed and put to bed, and all their wounds dressed," she wrote a few days later to her good friend Dr. Bowman in England.

"We have now *four miles* of beds, and not eighteen inches apart. . . ."

But this was not the end of the flood of sick and wounded —only the beginning.

Supply Officer Extraordinary

"The wounded are now lying up to our very door," Florence wrote in a letter home. They lay crowded in the two corridors, between the nurses' tower and the main gate, because the four wards were filled to capacity. "We are landing 540 more," she added.

Sick and wounded . . . sick and wounded . . . They came in a never-ending stream. If so many of them had not died, the new arrivals would have had to lie outdoors. In the hospital they ran out of mattress bags and straw. The wounded were laid upon the bare floors, with their boots under their heads—if they had boots. They were wrapped in their blood-stiffened coats—if they were lucky enough to have coats.

Battles did not account for all these casualties and hardships. Much of this suffering was the result of official mistakes which went on all through the campaign.

The Russians still held their naval base, Sevastopol. The British Army, commanded by Lord Raglan, camped on the heights above the seaport, their supply camp seven miles below, at Balaclava.

The November battle at Inkerman had been won by the

British, but again with a terrible loss of men. Several grim facts became obvious. The Russians had no intention of surrendering. Their position was still strong, and it was clear at this point that no quick victory could be gained. The British troops were exhausted, winter was setting in, and the soldiers were not prepared for the bone-chilling cold.

When the troops were first landed on the peninsula in October, the heat had been stifling. The seven-mile march to the heights was so grueling that the officers ordered the men to abandon their packs along the way. These packs contained everything a soldier needed, yet no provision was made to bring these up to the campsite later.

Now, in November, the weather changed suddenly—and the men had only their mud-caked summer uniforms. There was no proper shelter for them, no warm blankets, no warm clothes—not even enough food. The army could not withdraw from its position on the heights, nor could it get enough supplies brought up. The dirt roads had become rivers of mud.

The sanitary conditions became so bad that soon hundreds of soldiers were stricken with cholera.

Every bed in the army hospitals in the Crimea was filled. The men who did not die at the camp or down at the base were carried by ship to Scutari. Florence's nurses had more than enough to keep them busy now. And Florence, who was supposed to be their lady superintendent and direct their activities, now worked in the wards. She also assisted at the operations and amputations. These were still usually performed without anesthesia, in the wards and corridors, in sight of all the other men.

Many men died of fevers and the wound infections that followed every operation. Antiseptic methods and sterile hospital conditions were still years away. It was a miracle that anyone survived the surgery.

"Oh, you gentlemen of England," Florence wrote Dr. Bow-man, "you can have little idea, from reading the newspapers, of the horror and misery (in a military hospital) of operating on these dying, exhausted men. A London hospital is a garden of flowers compared to this."

The work of Florence and her nurses did not pass unnoticed. One young doctor was especially impressed.

"I could use a hundred nurses like them," he told Florence. "No, two hundred. It's a blessing you've come at a time like this. We could never have managed."

To Florence, his words were a blessing. She knew Dr. McGrigor worked with no thought of sparing himself.

"You have been on your feet more than twenty-four hours," she reminded him gently.

"These men have been suffering longer than that. I can't stop now," he told her, then added, with a weary smile, "You have not rested much yourself, Miss Nightingale."

That was true. But the hospital was filled and still more men kept arriving. How could she rest!

One day, as Florence passed through a ward, Sister Margaret Goodman hurried to her. "Miss Nightingale, some of the men who have just arrived refuse to let us help them. They say they are so filthy their own mothers wouldn't touch them. If only we could give them some clean clothes!"

But there were no clean clothes, no supplies, no fresh food. Bitterly, Flo thought of the ship from England, the *Prince,* that had steamed right past Scutari though it was loaded with desperately needed supplies for the hospital. It went on to the Crimea instead, to deliver ammunition. Now they would have to wait until the *Prince* returned.

Whenever she passed a window, Florence looked out at the Strait of Bosporus, hoping to catch sight of the ship. On Tuesday, November 14, she thought the Strait was unusually rough, and the tides remarkably high.

That night she and Selina were awakened by a strange, thrumming wind.

"What can it mean?" Selina asked.

Florence shook her head. "This area is subject to sudden shifts in weather. It can mean anything—but certainly a storm somewhere."

For a long time she lay awake worrying about the men in the wards and corridors, and thinking of the many broken windows that had not yet been repaired. If only they had more blankets. . . . But until the *Prince* returned, no one at the hospital seemed to know of any way to get the things needed by the men. When Florence asked Dr. Menzies, he referred her to Major Sillery. The major in turn looked distressed, but said it was not his department. Therefore, it was not his responsibility, according to army regulations. He sent her to old Mr. Ward.

Mr. Ward, who was at least seventy, was called a purveyor. He was in charge of buying and distributing supplies. He was polite, but firm.

"According to regulations," he said, "the men are supposed to bring their packs with them to the hospital. In the packs they have a change of clothing, eating utensils, razors, combs, brushes, soap—all the things you are requiring of me now, Miss Nightingale."

"The men have no packs," Florence pointed out. "You know as well as I that they were *ordered* to abandon them in the field."

"Nevertheless," Mr. Ward insisted, "I have no signed orders to replace anything. So you see, I can do nothing."

Florence saw, only too well. Everyone in charge was so tied and bound in the red tape of regulations that no one dared make an independent move. Yet it was obvious to everyone that this was an emergency, that men were dying for want of necessities. Well, in a few days the *Prince* would be returning, and then there would be some relief for this impossible situation.

But a few days later, Charles Bracebridge appeared before Florence with terrible news. "The *Prince* and all the supplies have been lost."

Selina covered her face with her hands and wept.

Florence gazed out of the window while she fought for self-control. "How did it happen?" she asked at last.

"Remember the strange wind and the high tides on the fourteenth?" Charles said. "There was a hurricane, the worst they've seen in years on the Peninsula. Not a tent is left standing. They say even horses were blown for miles. All the ships in Balaclava Harbor have been sunk, including the *Prince*."

Now the situation was more desperate than ever. Dr. Menzies found it impossible to provide even the simplest necessities for his patients. The men themselves seemed to have given up hope, and the wards were strangely, heartbreakingly quiet. At this point, Florence Nightingale decided to take matters into her own hands.

She knew that a Mr. Macdonald had been sent out by the London *Times* to supervise the spending of all the money— the thousands of pounds—collected by his paper for the relief of the soldiers. She also knew that so far no one had bothered to accept what he had to offer. Florence asked Charles Bracebridge to arrange a meeting for her with this gentleman at once.

Mr. Macdonald had seen Florence in action in the wards. When Charles brought him to the nurses' tower, Mr. Macdonald immediately put himself at Miss Nightingale's disposal.

"I felt sure that I could count on your cooperation," Florence told him. "I, too, have a large sum of money with me. Thirty thousand pounds, donated by people anxious to change this terrible situation. But the hospital officials say they must get their supplies from England. *Regulations*, you know," she added wryly. "I suggest that we can obtain what is necessary right here."

"No question about it!" Mr. Macdonald assured Flo. "I can get everything you need in Constantinople. It's one of the largest markets in the world. If you'll trust me to do the purchasing, I'll go to Constantinople this very morning."

Florence handed over the list she had ready. It was a long one. The first item was two hundred scrubbing brushes— and sackcloth for the cleaning of the hospital walls and floors. Then there was warm woolen clothing for the men, knives, forks, spoons, tin cups, towels, and soap.

Carefully Mr. Macdonald checked off Flo's lists for food, tables, trays, clocks, scissors for the trimming of the men's hair, fine-toothed combs and a solution for destroying lice.

She also wanted operating tables, so the patients would not be laid upon rickety boards set on trestles. And she ordered screens for the operating tables, so the poor fellows waiting to be operated on would not see the sufferings of their comrades. "The terrible impression puts such fear into their minds, it lessens their chances of survival," she told him.

When urgently needed supplies suddenly began to appear, the doctors stared in wonder. It did not take them long to discover where they came from. But so desperate was the situation that the doctors accepted everything and asked no questions. Soon Miss Nightingale became known as the unofficial purveyor, or supply officer, for anything needed. The words "Go to Miss Nightingale" were as powerful a charm as "Open Sesame." She always managed to have or to find anything required, and with the least possible delay. However, she never allowed anything to be issued from her private stores without a signed request from the medical officers.

No food from her stores was ever given to any patient under any circumstances without a specific order from the doctor in charge. This often angered the nurses. But Florence knew this was the proper course to take. Nurses must always act under doctors' orders. Otherwise fatal errors might be made. Florence had no intention of breaking any hospital rules.

Her first step, when a request came in, was to check with Mr. Ward. If he said the item was not in stock, she added it to her "shopping" list. Mr. Macdonald then fetched it from Constantinople.

Mr. Ward was heard to complain bitterly that Miss Nightingale never gave him enough *time* to get anything. She was always rushing off to get whatever was wanted on her own. But Florence was well aware that Mr. Ward's idea of time meant weeks or months—or never.

Once Florence received an order for warm shirts for the men at Balaclava. She knew that a shipment of 27,000 shirts had been sent from England, at her suggestion. They had arrived, but the purveyor said he could not unpack them until the Board of Survey inspected and released them. Florence promptly had similar shirts bought and shipped from Constantinople, while old Mr. Ward fumed in Scutari. After all, he complained, she could have had the Government shirts in three weeks or so. The fact that the soldiers lay half-naked and shivering and needed the shirts immediately was beside the point. Mr. Ward insisted that Miss Nightingale behaved in a most irregular and unmilitary manner.

On another occasion Miss Nightingale caused the purveyor even greater anguish. This time she informed him that she had the authority to have a Government shipment opened at her command. While the old man stood by, wringing his hands, Florence had the seals broken and took whatever was required, listing every single item in her records.

The responsibility which Florence Nightingale had assumed increased the comings and goings in the nurses' tower. Now orderlies with doctors' requests were always waiting at the door of her small office. A member of her staff checked each request to see that it was properly signed and countersigned before any supplies were given out.

Her staff called their quarters the Tower of Babel. At all hours everything and everyone seemed to be there—boxes, parcels, bundles of sheets, shirts, old linen and flannels, tubs of butter, sugar, bread, kettles, saucepans—besides the special diets which were being cooked and served.

Under Miss Nightingale's direction, and at her insistence, the wards were finally cleaned. Next she turned her attention to the washing of the men's clothes and bedding.

She rented a Turkish house nearby, and had hot-water boilers installed. Then she hired the soldiers' wives to do the washing.

The presence of the wives in Scutari was another of the Government's blunders. The Crimean campaign was supposed to have been a very short one—three weeks or so. And somehow two hundred wives were allowed to come out with their soldier husbands. But no provision for their housing or care was made. The poor women, and their children, lived in utter squalor in the dank, dark, filthy cellars of the Barrack Hospital.

With the aid of the faithful Bracebridges, Florence did what she could for them, but she was already under a crushing load of work and responsibility. Fortunately, Lady Alicia Blackwood came to Scutari with her missionary husband at just the right moment.

With Flo's help and advice, Lady Alicia found better quarters for the women. She established a hospital for them, supervised the work of some in the laundry, and set others to making bandages and hospital dressings. Eventually she started a school for the children. Both Lady Alicia and the Reverend Dr. Blackwood were a great help to Flo.

The two hospitals in Scutari were beginning to emerge from chaos into some sort of order. But both were still terribly overcrowded. Then, early in December, the commander-in-chief of the army, Lord Raglan, sent word that five hundred more patients were being shipped to Scutari.

The medical staff was aghast.

"We can't possibly cram another man into these wards or corridors," Dr. McGrigor said. "If only we had the use of the burned-out wing of this place! But I suppose there isn't any money to repair it. And no one would have the authority to order the construction."

Florence looked out across the open court at the fourth side of the huge square that formed the Barrack Hospital. This section of the hospital had been badly gutted by fire before the British arrived. But she knew that there was space for two large wards. And with the corridor between the wards, there would be room for almost a thousand additional patients. The repairs would be costly—and the red tape almost endless. Still, it could be done.

"Our ambassador here, Lord Stratford, has all the money and authority that's needed," Florence told Dr. McGrigor. Had not Sidney Herbert assured her again and again that Lord Stratford had been directed to spare no expense for the well-being of the British soldiers?

Dr. McGrigor laughed shortly. "The ambassador? Miss Nightingale, you can't be serious. He lives in that palace of his in plain sight of this hospital. He knows full well the difficulties we've had. And he has not lifted a finger to help!"

"I shall ask him nevertheless," Florence declared.

An Unwelcome Addition

Miss Nightingale immediately sent a message to the ambassador, stating the urgent situation at the Barrack Hospital. To everyone's surprise, 125 Turkish men were hired to build the wards in the burned-out section. But it was a short-lived triumph. After a few days the workers decided their pay was too low and they went on strike. Florence wrote to the ambassador. The ambassador said there was nothing he could do.

Once more Florence acted independently. She went out and hired 200 men, on her own responsibility. Again she paid for the workers and the materials with private funds.

And so "the wards were ready to receive the 500 men from the ships *Ripon* and *Golden Fleece*," Florence reported to Sidney Herbert.

The soldiers were in the last stages of exhaustion—cold, weak, starved, and filthy. They were quickly washed, given clean clothes, and put into clean beds. These beds were set on wooden stands, raised about a foot from the floor—built at the direction of Miss Nightingale. No sooner were the men settled than her nurses hurried in with warm food—arrowroot, ladled out of huge milk pails, containing generous portions of port wine. Florence had supplied all the utensils for this wing, since the purveyor could provide nothing. Her contribution included "knives, forks, spoons, cans, towels, etc.," she wrote Mr. Herbert.

After the hardships endured at Balaclava and aboard ship, the soldiers could scarcely believe their good fortune. One of them said, "We felt we were in heaven."

The doctors at Scutari had nothing but praise for Florence Nightingale. On the Peninsula, however, some of the officers were resentful of her "high-handed" actions. Her boldness in the face of regulations shocked them. It was unheard of— most irregular. How dared she spend all that money without consulting anyone! Surely now the Government would set her down.

Instead, Miss Nightingale received complete approval from the War Department. Moreover, every penny she spent was refunded to her. This demonstration of "the Nightingale power" made a tremendous impression on everyone, and her position was greatly strengthened.

As usual, her concern was not with personal glory and power. Her primary mission was still to prove the value of women as nurses. Although the nurses were busy enough now, the quality of their work and their personal behavior often caused her considerable anxiety.

Of her original group of thirty-eight nurses, Florence had found sixteen women who were really dependable. Six of these were exceptional. Mrs. Roberts, from St. Thomas's Hospital in London, was "worth her weight in gold." Mrs. Drake, from St. John's House, was "a treasure." And of course there was the Reverend Mother from Bermondsey and her nuns. They were Florence's faithful supporters in every endeavor. But among the others, one nurse had been sent home already for improper conduct . . . and there were two more who must be dismissed . . . and there was Mrs. Lawfield.

Flo had a keen sense of humor and was able to see the

funny side of many situations. All her life it was this ability that helped her through bitter disappointments, appalling situations—and the Mrs. Lawfields of her world.

"I came out, ma'am, prepared to submit to everything, to be put upon in every way. But there are some things, ma'am, one can't submit to. . . ." Flo's lips twitched in amusement as she recalled how plump, elderly Mrs. Lawfield's bosom rose and fell with agitation as she had faced her in the office some days ago. "There is the *caps*, ma'am, that suits one face and some that suits another. And if I'd known, ma'am, about the caps, great as was my desire to come out to nurse at Scutari, I wouldn't have come, ma'am."

Despite that heated speech, Mrs. Lawfield was turning into a truly able nurse. Under the stress of real emergencies, she had become resigned to her cap. Perhaps the other women— when she had weeded out the unfit—would also turn into reliable nurses. But it was so hard to instill discipline . . . the strict obedience to orders . . . the need for personal conduct beyond reproach. . . .

Flo sighed. There was her sense of mission about nursing. Then, too, she felt a strong responsibility to Sidney Herbert. If they failed, he would be blamed for sending women out to military hospitals.

And yet, Flo thought, she had every right to a feeling of satisfaction at the way things were going now. So much good had come of their being here. The lines of her mouth softened as she thought of the hundreds of men lying in the wards and corridors all around this tower. She was beginning to think of them as her "children." They were so brave. They bore the pain of their dreadful wounds, disease, and privations with such heroism, without complaints. And they were so touchingly grateful for every attention.

With a soft swish of her full black merino skirt, Florence settled herself at the small unpainted table in the room she shared with Selina Bracebridge. She adjusted the wick of the lamp and the light glowed on her delicate, earnest face. Her chestnut hair was almost hidden under her plain white cap. She tied a black kerchief over the cap and wrapped her wool shawl more tightly about her shoulders. It was so cold and damp in Scutari and they never had enough fuel. Florence hated the cold, but she would not allow herself to think about it. She dipped her quill pen into the ink bottle and prepared to write Sidney Herbert of their accomplishments thus far. "14 December, 1854 . . ."

Florence and Selina carried on a huge and necessary correspondence, and reserved the quiet hours of the night for the reading and writing of letters. "Do you realize, Selina," said Florence, "that we have already supplied the men with two thousand shirts?"

Selina Bracebridge did not seem to hear. She was absorbed in a letter which trembled in her hands.

Florence's cheerful voice went on. "We've stirred up the whole machinery here, and the doctors are really counting on us for assistance. I'm telling Sidney how the best of our nurses are attending to hundreds of daily dressings and compound fractures, and giving out medicines at the proper times. Do you remember, when we came here, the orderlies used to give patients the medicines prescribed for the whole day all at once! I do believe that we've succeeded in—" She turned, and broke off suddenly at sight of her companion's face.

Selina Bracebridge was staring at her with a stunned expression.

Instantly Florence was at her side. "What is it? What's wrong?"

"This letter—from Liz Herbert," Selina answered thickly. "It—it seems that Mary Stanley and a party of forty-six nurses will be arriving here—tomorrow."

It was Florence's turn to look stunned.

"Mary Stanley!" she exclaimed. "But she has no practical

knowledge of nursing. Why would she be coming? She
helped collect our party in London—but now, for her to bring
out forty-six more women—Selina, I did not *ask* for more
nurses!"

Selina shook her head. "They are not assigned to you, Flo.
Liz Herbert says they're to report to Dr. Cumming, at the
General Hospital here."

The color drained from Florence's face, then rushed back
as if she had been slapped. There must be some mistake. This
was not possible. Selina put Liz Herbert's letter into Flo's
icy hand. Flo scanned it with a sense of overwhelming shock.

What did this mean? How could more nurses be sent out
without consulting her? Had she somehow been discredited
in the eyes of the Government? Was the War Office displeased with her work? Was her appointment as Superintendent of Nurses in Scutari withdrawn in this outrageous,
humiliating, public fashion without a word of explanation?

Hurt and bewildered, Flo wrote Sidney Herbert a long,
blistering letter. She reminded him that he had stated, in a
document made public through the newspapers, that *no additional nurses would be sent out to Scutari until she asked
for them.*

She reminded him of something else, too, of how she had
wanted to take with her only a carefully selected group of
twenty. Instead she wrote, "I sacrificed my own judgment and
went out with forty females, well knowing that half that
number would be more efficient and less trouble. . . ."

This was still such a new, uncertain experiment—having
untrained women working among some 3,000 soldiers. It was
so difficult to control them. . . .

Flo dipped her pen again and went on writing. "Experience has justified my foreboding. But I have toiled my way
into the confidence of the medical men. I have, by incessant
vigilance, day and night, introduced something like order into

the work of these women. And the plan may be said to have succeeded."

Wryly Flo recalled her own happy mood, now shattered. Her pen moved on, reproaching Sidney Herbert for his thoughtless action. The sending of a "fresh batch of women at no one's requisition, and raising our number to eighty-four. . . ."

Where could they put them? "The quartering of them *here* is a physical impossibility, the employment of them a moral impossibility . . . ," she wrote. She simply could not take the time now to train these new females. Goodness knew who and what they were! She did not have much faith in Mary Stanley's judgment. And past experience led her to believe that the newcomers' total nursing skills would not amount to much. It would be extraordinary good luck if three or four proved really capable. As for their personal conduct— Flo shuddered. Since she had not been formally removed as the lady superintendent, *she* would be held accountable for these women, regardless of who brought them out. And Liz Herbert's letter said they were not to report to her! Again the quill raced across the pages.

"You have sacrificed the cause, so dear to my heart," she wrote Mr. Herbert. "You have sacrificed me—a matter of small importance now. You have sacrificed your own written word to a popular cry. . . ."

Florence stared at that last sentence. Hurt and angry though she was, at that moment Flo began to suspect the possible reason behind this shipment of unwanted nurses. Enthusiastic reports about her mission had been sent to England. One of the chaplains at Scutari, a friend of the Herberts, had written, "As for Miss Nightingale and her companions, nothing can be said too strong in their praise. She works them wonderfully, and they are so useful that I have no hesitation in saying some twenty more of the same sort would be a very great blessing to the establishment. . . ."

The people at home were clamoring for more and better care for their sick and wounded soldiers. They had no idea of the difficulties that Miss Nightingale had to meet, or of the responsibility she had to shoulder when she sent her nurses into the wards.

Sidney Herbert, overworked and pressed on all sides, gave in when Mary Stanley offered her services. Somehow he had agreed to send her. And by having her report to Dr. Cumming, he must have thought it would be less trouble for Flo. This might even have been suggested to him by Mary Stanley, who was ambitious, impulsive, and jealous of Florence's growing fame. Miss Stanley had no wish to be placed under Florence's authority. And, like many other ladies in England, she had rather romantic—and totally impractical—notions about the nursing of the soldiers.

Instead of easing Florence's burden, this arrangement threatened to undermine the authority and respect she had worked so hard to develop. By casting serious doubts upon her backing from the Government, everything she had managed to accomplish so far was in danger of being destroyed.

Were all her dreams doomed to failure? Was opposition and frustration to be her lot always? Florence experienced deep despair as she waited for the arrival of the Stanley party.

On December 15, 1854, the *Egypt* dropped anchor in the harbor at Constantinople. Shortly thereafter, Charles Bracebridge went on board to see Mary Stanley.

He and Selina had known her for a long time. And Charles was depending now on these friendships to help him convince Mary that she must return to England. If Mary insisted on landing at Scutari, Florence Nightingale would resign. Charles could not bear the thought that this might happen. Surely Mary Stanley would understand.

She came to him at once, extending her hand graciously. "Ah, Mr. Bracebridge! How kind of you to escort us to Scutari," she exclaimed. "How is dear Flo?"

"She is quite well," Charles replied, "but terribly overworked." It was the wrong thing to say.

Miss Stanley looked concerned. "The very reason we have come, my dear Charles. We've read all the accounts in *The Times*. Flo has become quite a romantic heroine. Everyone in London is talking about her. We want to do what we can to help."

Charles gazed at Miss Stanley steadily. This woman had very little understanding of the work Florence was doing, or of the long-range results she hoped to gain with it. He tried to explain—but he was no diplomat.

"Flo deserves the admiration," he said. "Actually, the work in the hospital is far from romantic. It's grim, heartbreaking labor. Flo and her nurses endure incredible hardships under terribly crowded conditions. The situation is so bad that I have come to ask you a favor."

Miss Stanley's eyes glowed with pleasure. "My dear Charles, anything at all for Flo."

"Then go back, please. There is no room at the hospital. Our party of forty is crowded into a space of less than five rooms. Our water is rationed. Food is scarce. Flo finds it difficult to supervise the nurses she already has. The best thing you can do for her is go back."

"Go back!" Miss Stanley bridled. "We wouldn't think of it. Surely Flo didn't send you to ask us to return to England!" Her eyes narrowed.

Charles shook his head.

"Well, then!" Mary Stanley shrugged. "Anyway, Flo won't have to bother about us, dear Charles. I intend to supervise my own nurses."

Charles did not give up yet. He warned Miss Stanley of the opposition of the medical officers. He reminded her that

Sidney Herbert had given Florence the position of Superintendent of Nurses. Miss Stanley's smile became icy.

"You forget that I came here at Sidney Herbert's request. Can you deny that there is a desperate need for competent nurses here?" she demanded.

This Charles could not do. Yet, competent nursing was the very key to the problem.

Miss Stanley's party had been gathered hastily. It was composed of fifteen nuns, twenty-two paid nurses, and nine ladies. Most of the nuns had no hospital experience, and most of the nurses were not women of the highest character. And the ladies, like Miss Stanley, had the romantic idea that their mere presence would inspire the soldiers to recover. Charles knew they would find it difficult to deal with the ugly realities of nursing at Scutari. He was certain they would only cause trouble and confirm the poor opinion the doctors had of hospital nurses in general.

Discouraged, he left the ship and reported to Florence and Selina. Florence had spent hours on her knees dressing wounds. More sick men were arriving from the Crimea. Yesterday there had been two hundred, today many more. The death rate rose alarmingly.

When Selina saw Charles, she hurried toward him hopefully. He shook his head and Selina knew that he had failed. Mary Stanley was here to stay.

"But there's no room! They will *have* to go back," cried Selina.

"They'll go to the ambassador and he'll provide for them— for now," Charles said. "After all, Sidney Herbert sent them."

Florence listened thoughtfully. She had not quite finished her letter to Sidney Herbert. Tonight, after making her rounds of the wards and corridors, she would complete what she had to say to him.

It was after midnight when she took up her pen again. "You must feel that I ought to resign," she wrote sadly, adding that she would remain at her post till he appointed a new superintendent in her place, "until which time I will continue to discharge my duties as well as I can."

"Shall I post that letter for you, Flo?" Selina asked the next morning.

Florence hesitated. She did not want to leave Scutari. There was so much to be done. She fingered the letter, then put the envelope aside without sealing it. "Not yet," she replied. "Just take the others, please."

Three days later she had not changed her mind about anything in the letter. To make certain that Mr. Herbert would not think she had written in haste, she added a line at the bottom: "Written 15 December. Posted 18 December."

The letter was mailed. It would take nearly two weeks to reach Sidney Herbert—and as long again to hear from him.

Miss Stanley and her nurses began almost immediately to cause trouble. When they reported to Dr. Cumming at the General Hospital, he flatly refused to employ them. When they offered to help in the Barrack Hospital, the doctors did not want them either. And when Miss Stanley's group learned of the strict rules Miss Nightingale had established for all nurses, they rebelled.

"Flo expects entirely too much in the way of discipline," Miss Stanley complained.

It was, of course, this very discipline which had won the medical staff's approval. Now, as Miss Stanley's women began to appear where they were not wanted, the medical officers began to wonder: perhaps allowing "petticoats" into army hospitals was a mistake after all.

Although Miss Nightingale's influence suffered setbacks in Scutari, in England her position was considerably strengthened by Queen Victoria herself. Early in December the Queen wrote to Sidney Herbert:

"Would you tell Mrs. Herbert that I beg her to let me see the accounts she receives from Miss Nightingale and Mrs. Bracebridge, as I hear *no details of the wounded* though I see so many from officers etc., about the battlefield and naturally the former must interest *me* more than anyone. Let Mrs. Herbert also know that I wish Miss Nightingale and the ladies would tell those poor noble wounded and sick men that *no one* takes a warmer interest or feels *more* for their sufferings or admires their courage and heroism *more* than their Queen. Day and night she thinks of her beloved troops. So does the Prince. Beg Mrs. Herbert to communicate these my words to those ladies, as I know that *our* sympathy is valued by these noble fellows."

The Queen's message arrived shortly before Christmas and the chaplains went through the wards and corridors, reading it to the men. Copies were posted in the hospitals and published in the newspapers. The men were deeply touched.

"To think of *her* thinking of *us!*" a soldier marveled.

"Each man of us ought to have a copy to keep with him till his dying day," said another.

"I only wish I could go and fight for her again," a badly wounded man whispered hoarsely.

The Queen followed up her message with visible proof of her interest in the men. Bales of gifts arrived for them, along with a personal message for Miss Nightingale. Her Majesty wanted Florence to distribute the gifts herself, as she would know where each item would prove the most useful. Also, the Queen wanted Miss Nightingale to know that *her* goodness and self-devotion in giving of herself "to the soothing attendance upon these wounded and sick soldiers had been observed by the Queen with sentiments of the highest approval and admiration." Was there something else the Queen could do for her soldiers?

Yes, there was! For some time now Florence had been

trying to get an increase in the sick pay for the soldiers. She wrote the Queen directly about this, and the result was like a fairy tale: "No sooner said, than done."

In Scutari the astonished officials could only wonder at the extent of Miss Nightingale's influence. She could get what she wanted straight from the Queen!

During the second week of January, 1855, Florence received an answer to her letter. Sidney Herbert acknowledged the mistake he had made in sending Mary Stanley. He assured Flo that he had meant only to relieve her of some of the wearisome work. Her "experiment" had proved so successful that he felt more nurses would be welcome—especially since there were so many sick and wounded. In the letter he not only reconfirmed her authority but begged her not to resign. Moreover, he left all decisions regarding the Stanley group to Flo's judgment. Mr. Herbert said further, "If you see fit, send Miss Stanley and her party home at my personal expense."

By this time Florence had been able to view the situation more calmly. It might do more harm than good to send the newcomers back—especially since there were excellent nurses among them. Therefore she added some Stanley nurses to her own staff, and sent home several of her own group who had proved incompetent.

At the end of January, Lord Raglan suggested that some of the Stanley nurses be sent to the Crimea. The others, he thought, should go to a new hospital at Koulali, five miles up the Bosporus. Mary Stanley was to organize the nursing staff there. Miss Stanley set off haughtily for Koulali and promptly established the "lady" plan of nursing there. Maids were hired to do the disagreeable tasks while the ladies went about the wards cheering up the men and brewing little pots of tea and delicacies for their favorite patients.

Miss Stanley, however, did not "lady" it for long at Koulali.

When the first 300 sick and wounded soldiers were landed, she was faced with the reality of filth, infection, and open wounds. She became hysterical, claimed that her health could not stand the strain, and soon left for home.

And so this ordeal ended for Florence Nightingale. She was more firmly established than ever as the lady-in-chief at Scutari. But she had neither time nor inclination to bask in triumph. The cruel winter was decimating the British Army. Men fell ill or died by the hundreds. By January 1855 there were 11,000 soldiers in the camp above Sevastopol—and 12,000 in the army hospitals! Shipload after shipload, the sick arrived at Scutari.

It was, Flo wrote Mr Herbert, "calamity unparalleled in the history of calamity."

The Lady with the Lamp

IN THIS new emergency, everyone turned to Florence Nightingale. She alone appeared calm in the face of disaster. Even the purveyors—the supply officers—now came to her, pleading for the things she alone could secure without delay.

"Nursing," she wrote Sidney Herbert, "is the least of the functions into which I have been forced."

And yet, despite the staggering load of responsibility, she found time for the nursing, too. She had an uncanny way of knowing where she was needed most. And there she went— to comfort a desperately ill new arrival, or perhaps to assist with an amputation. The patient, looking up to find the lady-in-chief at his side, standing firm, willing herself to witness the pain, willing *him* to bear it, found new courage and strength as a soldier.

Few soldiers at Scutari died alone. Florence sat at the bedsides of at least two thousand dying men herself. She took down their last words to their families. This included a promise to help the bereaved wife and children—a promise faithfully kept through Flo's relatives or friends at home. Often the financial help was provided by Florence herself.

There was no use telling her to save her strength or herself.

Florence Nightingale would spend eight hours on her knees dressing wounds. Or stand for twenty hours supervising the admission of patients, distributing supplies, or, with utter disregard for the danger to herself from the infections, nursing men with typhus and gangrene.

Then the deadly Asiatic cholera broke out. It was so virulent that in three weeks seven doctors, three nurses, and old Mr. Ward, the purveyor, died of the disease.

Florence Nightingale drove herself mercilessly. Yet she never felt she was doing enough.

She even managed to write the special reports—some of them thirty pages long—that Sidney Herbert requested. Sitting in her frigid little office, Florence must have worn down hundreds of quill pens as her small, cold hand raced across the pages.

She sent Sidney Herbert a detailed and practical scheme for reorganizing army hospitals. She also urged that a sanitary commission be sent out from England to inspect the army hospitals and camps. In spite of all the cleaning and improved conditions, at the Barrack Hospital in particular, something was terribly wrong. The death rate was mounting continuously.

Flo wrote Sidney Herbert, "I work in the wards all day and write all night." Her light was seen burning at all hours, and often her head would drop over her work in utter exhaustion. Then Selina and Charles Bracebridge would carry her slight form to her narrow bed and cover her. There for a few hours she would sleep like one dead.

The troops adored Florence. "If the Queen was to die," said a victim of the Battle of Alma, "they ought to make *her* Queen, and I think they would."

They thought she would make a good general, too. "If she was at the head there," they said, "we would be in Sevastopol in a week!"

The men never knew her own troubled thoughts, her

weariness, her despair. "She was all full of life and fun when she talked to us," they said, "especially if a man was a bit downhearted."

"Before she came," another veteran reported, "there was cussing and swearing. But after that it was holy as a church." No man would risk offending the Lady's ears.

Florence did not feel it was wise for her nurses to be in the wards after eight at night. Instead, when all was quiet, she would make her final tour of the hospital. A new volunteer, who was permitted to go with her once, wrote that it seemed like an endless, but never-to-be-forgotten walk. She and Florence went around the whole of the second story of the huge Barrack Hospital, into many of the wards, and into one of the upper corridors. "As we slowly passed along, the silence was profound," wrote this lady. "Very seldom did a moan or cry from those deeply suffering ones fall on our ears. A dim light burned here and there. Miss Nightingale carried her lantern, which she would set down before she bent over any of the patients. I much admired her manner to the men—it was so tender and kind."

In the long dark corridors, the light of her lamp brought hope to the suffering men.

"Her very presence was like magic," the doctors reported. "The men became heroic for her sake."

One night, as she was about to start on her rounds, Florence was surprised to find a boy sitting outside her door. He appeared to be no more than twelve. When he saw her, he rose unsteadily to his feet. Florence recognized him as Tommy, the drummer boy who had been brought in a few weeks before suffering from exposure.

"Child, why aren't you in bed?" she asked him.

The lad drew himself up to his full height. "I come to carry the lamp, Lady. Please, I'm strong enough now. I can help you."

He was so eager that Florence smiled. The child might have a cheering effect on the men, too, she thought. "Very well, Thomas. I do need someone to help me with the lamp," she told him. "Thank you for thinking of it." The tall, slim woman and the boy set out down the long, chilly corridor together.

After that Tommy slept outside the door to the nurses' quarters. He kept Miss Nightingale's desk lamp and her camp lantern clean and always ready to use.

Thousands of the men in the British Army felt Florence Nightingale's influence. Their letters home were filled with stories about her, and her name became a byword in English homes. One letter became very famous and was passed from hand to hand: "What a comfort it was to see her pass even. She would speak to one and nod and smile to as many more; but she could not do it all, you know. We lay there by the hundreds. But we would kiss her shadow as it fell, and lay our heads on the pillow again, content."

Word of Flo's effect on the men reached not only England but elsewhere in the world. Poems and tributes of every kind were written to her. The American poet Longfellow wrote the lines which have become the most famous of all:

> Lo! in that hour of misery
> A lady with a lamp I see
> > Pass through the glimmering gloom,
> > And flit from room to room.
> And slow, as in a dream of bliss,
> The speechless sufferer turns to kiss
> Her shadow, as it falls
> Upon the darkening walls.

While Florence Nightingale was being idolized in England, the same public furiously blamed the Government for all the ills that befell the soldiers. As a result of such criticism, there was a change in the Government leadership. A new Prime

Minister came into office and Sidney Herbert was no longer
Secretary at War.

The new Prime Minister, Lord Palmerston, was a neighbor
of the Nightingales at Embley. He was Florence's old friend
and supporter. The new Secretary of State for War, Lord
Panmure, was instructed, therefore, to give every considera-
tion and prompt attention to Miss Nightingale's requests. So,
in England, at least, there were no obstacles to Florence's
work. Her reports were forwarded to the Queen as before.
And though Sidney Herbert was no longer in the Government, he had no intention of giving up his efforts to improve
conditions in the army. He urged Florence to continue to send
letters and reports to him. Her suggestions would be forwarded to the proper people.

Finally, at the end of February, one of Florence's most
important requests was granted. The new Prime Minister
sent a sanitary commission to the war zone. The commission
was instructed not only to *investigate* conditions in Scutari
and on the Crimea, but to *do* something about them *at once*.
And they did. After six months of frustration, everything
Florence had pleaded for suddenly began to get done.

The first thing the commission discovered was the source
of the foul stench in the Barrack Hospital, which could be
smelled *outside* the walls. Beneath this building there were
open sewers and cesspools choked with filth. The plaster
walls were soaked with it. The decaying mass sent up something much worse than the smell—a poisonous gas—into
every ward and corridor. The water supply was found to be
contaminated, too. It was mixed with sewage—and when the
channel was dug up, it was found that the drinking water
had been filtering through the body of a dead horse.

The fact that disease was spread by bacteria, germs, and
viruses had not yet been discovered. But intelligent people
knew that somehow dirt and foul air spread infection. The

dirt had been cleared up to some extent since Miss Nightingale had taken charge. But the air in the Barrack Hospital was so sickening that visitors frequently fell ill from breathing it even for a few minutes! No wonder the death rate was so high. The wonder was that anyone survived.

Now the sanitary commission engaged an army of Turkish workers to clean out the sewers, wash the walls with lime, and get rid of the rats and the rubbish that littered the great courtyard and the whole camp surrounding the hospital. The hospital was disinfected, and the water supply purified.

The effect of all this was felt immediately. The death rate dropped at once. More men recovered from their illnesses. "The sanitary commission," Florence Nightingale said later, "saved the British Army."

And now spring came with a rush, bathing everything in warm, healing sunshine. Soon there were only 1100 cases in the Barrack Hospital—and of these, fewer than 100 were bed patients.

Florence now had another helper and enthusiastic admirer. This was Alexis Soyer, a French chef, long famous in England. Soyer had come out to Scutari at his own expense and brought with him his secretary-assistant, a quiet Negro gentleman. Mr. Soyer was dapper, talkative, and full of comic mannerisms. He was also a genius—and Miss Nightingale recognized this very quickly. "Others," she wrote a friend, "have studied cookery for the purpose of showy menus. . . . He for the purpose of cooking large quantities of food in the most nutritive and economical manner for great numbers of people."

Although Mr. Soyer was not welcomed by the officials, he came armed with authority to reform the Barrack kitchens, and he set to work at once. He trained soldiers to be cooks—something no one else had done before. He invented ovens and field stoves, and a "scutari teapot" which made and kept hot tea for fifty men. When he appeared in the wards, with his tureens of hot soup or tasty stews, the men cheered.

At long last Florence felt that the Barrack Hospital was in satisfactory condition. She was now able to give her attention to the hospitals in the Crimea. Reports about them were disturbing. The fight for Sevastopol was starting again and Florence felt keenly the need for better hospital care *close to the front*. Why should the wounded have to suffer the added agonies of going by ship down to Scutari? Florence also wanted to improve the diet kitchens in these hospitals with Mr. Soyer's help.

And there was always the problem of discipline among the nurses. The Crimean hospitals had small staffs of women, most of them from the Stanley party. The reports of the behavior of some were upsetting. These women had their own superintendents, who in turn were supposed to be responsible to Florence Nightingale. This was her understanding and certainly what the War Department had intended.

Dr. John Hall was the chief medical officer in the Crimea, but Florence had not yet met him. Dr. Hall was not anxious to meet *her*. She had revealed too manys of the weaknesses of the army hospital administration. Now that the sanitary commission had found so many faults, his pride was raw. It was all the fault of that meddling Bird, Florence Nightingale.

Florence had the approval of the War Office for her visit of inspection. But Dr. Hall insisted she had no business in the Crimea. Her appointment, he said, named her "Superintendent of the Female Nursing Establishment in the English Military Hospitals in *Turkey*." The Crimean Peninsula was in Russia. Therefore, Dr. Hall maintained, she had no authority in the Crimea.

Florence was upset by this new opposition, but she did not change her plans. She decided to leave Mrs. Bracebridge in charge at Scutari and to deal with Dr. Hall as best she could.

On May 2, 1855, she sailed from Scutari for Balaclava. She

took with her four nurses, including the invaluable Mrs. Roberts. Mr. Soyer and his assistant came on board loaded with kitchen gear. Mr. Bracebridge came, as usual, to help in any way he could, and brought an invalid soldier, Robert Robinson, to serve as a messenger. And twelve-year-old Tommy, the drummer boy, came too. He now called himself "Miss Nightingale's man" and would scarcely let Flo out of his sight.

Their ship arrived in Balaclava on May 5. Flo noticed that the decks of the many vessels in the harbor were crowded with people and others were putting out in small boats from the pier.

"Who are they?" Flo asked Charles Bracebridge, "Why have they gathered here?"

Mr. Bracebridge gazed quizzically at the modest lady-in-chief. "I imagine they've come here for a look at you," he told her.

Flo was dismayed. She did not seek personal glory. She did not want ceremonies and official greetings.

But already all sorts of important people were boarding the vessel. Mr. Soyer reported that it soon became a floating reception room, with doctors, senior officers, officials from various departments, including the sanitary commission, all crowding around Miss Nightingale. Eveyone who possibly could, came—except Dr. Hall.

The captain invited Miss Nightingale to make her head-quarters aboard ship, and she agreed.

That afternoon, escorted by a number of important gentle-men, she went ashore to report to Lord Raglan, commander-in-chief of the British forces. Florence was provided with a pretty mare to ride, so light brown in color that she appeared golden in the sun. It had been some time since Flo had ridden a horse, but she sat easily in the saddle on her lively mount.

When the party arrived at Lord Raglan's quarters, Florence

learned that he was away for the day. She decided to ride up and see the great guns trained down upon the port of Sevastopol. Many of the soldiers she had nursed in Scutari had come from this very spot.

The sight of a lady, riding a lively mare and accompanied by so many important gentlemen, some in glittering uniforms, astonished the soldiers. All at once they realized that here was Florence Nightingale herself! Men rushed from their tents to see her—the one person who had brought hope and comfort to them in these months of despair.

Florence was persuaded to sit on one of the cannons so that everyone could catch a glimpse of her. The men cheered her lustily, giving her the traditional British "three times three" salute. *"Hip, hip, hooray! Hip, hip, hooray!"* rang over the high plateau.

Some of the men began to gather bouquets of wild flowers that carpeted the plain. They asked her to choose the bouquet she liked best. Flo opened her arms and took them all.

Soon after this she remounted the mare and started down the steep slopes toward Balaclava. Now the strain of the day began to show. Florence's shoulders drooped in exhaustion. Uneasily Charles Bracebridge cantered to her side. "It's nothing, Charles," she said. "Just the unaccustomed fresh air."

Next morning she began her inspection of the hospitals. Immediately she was met with rudeness. Some of the nurses at the General Hospital in Balaclava, encouraged by Dr. Hall's hostility, did not even listen to her instructions.

For the sake of her work Florence could ignore both insolence and rudeness. However, nothing escaped her eyes—the dirt, the careless attitude toward the common soldiers, the disorganized diet kitchens.

Florence realized that she must quickly establish her authority with Dr. Hall. She would see him tomorrow.

But she felt unusually weary the next day—and then, suddenly, she collapsed. Several doctors were summoned and finally a bulletin was issued: Miss Nightingale was suffering from the Crimean fever, the disease which had killed so many of the soldiers she had nursed at Scutari.

"All Balaclava," reported Mr. Soyer, "was in an uproar."

She must be removed from the ship, the doctors advised, and taken to the Castle Hospital on the Heights.

A stretcher was prepared and relays of soldiers volunteered to carry it. Mrs. Roberts walked at Miss Nightingale's side. Mr. Soyer's secretary held an umbrella over Florence's head, to shield her from the sun. Robert Robinson, the invalid soldier-messenger, walked behind, tears streaming down his face. He was not strong enough to help carry the stretcher. And behind him trailed young Thomas, weeping bitterly because he was neither strong enough for the stretcher, nor tall enough to hold the umbrella for the Lady. But he still carried her lamp, stubbornly refusing to leave it behind on the ship. "She may have need of it yet," he said.

A few days later, word reached Scutari. "She's sick with the fever in Balaclava. They don't think she'll live." There was no need to ask who "she" was. Sad-faced soldiers told one another the news. The bedridden "turned their faces to the wall and cried," a sergeant wrote home. There were telltale smudges on his letter, too.

"All our trust was in her," the men said. "May God spare our gentle Lady with the Lamp."

Angel of the Crimea

FLORENCE HOVERED between life and death.

"Miss Nightingale's chances for recovery are very poor," her doctor reported. "She is a delicate woman and she has pushed herself far beyond her strength. Indeed, it is remarkable that she has not fallen ill before this."

The sad tidings streaked over the newly built telegraph lines and burst like a thunderclap in England. Miss Nightingale was ill . . . dying! It was a national calamity. Grieving people gathered in the streets, waiting for the latest news. At Embley, Parthe and her parents joined the villagers in prayers for Florence's recovery.

Meanwhile, in a hospital hut on the Heights in the Crimea, Flo was burning with fever and crying out in delirium. Young Tommy, forbidden to enter the hut, huddled as close as he could outside.

Poor Flo thought that the room was full of people demanding supplies from her. Her fever was so high that it seemed her frail, wasted form could not survive another moment. Then suddenly, for the first time in two weeks, Flo fell into a natural sleep.

On May 24, Lord Raglan telegraphed a welcome message to England. Miss Nightingale was out of danger!

She was advised to go home, and she agreed. But to her, "home" was Scutari. And as soon as she regained her strength, she intended to return to the Crimea.

The lady-in-chief was put aboard a private steam yacht. The rough passage across the Black Sea and the Bosporus exhausted her so that she was unable to speak or even feed herself. In Scutari, arrangements had been made for her to stay in the chaplain's house. At the pier, soldiers were ready to carry her stretcher. Many more waited to greet her and wish her well. When they saw how terribly changed she was, how pale and wasted, they stood in stricken silence. The men wept unashamedly as they followed the slowly moving stretcher up the hill. With a kind of loving fierceness, they fought to carry her baggage.

Her recovery was slow. But by July she had resumed her business correspondence. In August, 1855, she was back in her hospital quarters, and at work. She would not spare herself while there was so much still to be done.

During her convalescence Lord Raglan died, of the same terrible fever. Florence knew she had lost a good friend and supporter. The new commander-in-chief, General Simpson, was not sympathetic to Florence or to the work of her nurses. There was also a new senior medical officer at the Barrack Hospital—and he took his orders from Dr. Hall.

The other medical officers did not wish to side with Florence against Dr. Hall's man. Even young Dr. McGrigor no longer supported her.

"There is nothing more you can do here," he told her. "The hospital is running smoothly. Your nurses have proved themselves worthy. Why not return to England?"

Florence stared at him in disbelief. "Return! When there's so much more to be done?" How could he not see it!

Dr. McGrigor left her, shaking his head.

One of Florence's concerns was the welfare of the soldiers who were well enough to get around. Another was for the soldiers stationed at the camp in Scutari. There was nothing for them to do during their free hours but drink and gamble. Money which should have gone home to their families was spent almost as soon as the soldiers got their pay.

"What can you expect?" the officers told her. "These fellows come from the lowest classes. They are shiftless and ignorant. Most of them cannot even read or write."

Once Florence had retorted, "You vastly underestimate the British soldiers. If we gave them the opportunity to send money home, they would do so. If there were schools and reading rooms for them, they would spend far less time in gambling and drinking."

Florence Nightingale had come to the East to prove the value of women in nursing. Now she had another mission as well: to show the true worth of the British common soldier and to improve his lot.

With her usual efficiency, she began to draw up programs for the education and relaxation of the soldiers.

When her ideas were known in England, people responded at once. A great deal of money was raised and much was accomplished quickly.

Hundreds of cartons containing maps, illustrated books, plays, magazines, and newspapers were sent to the soldiers. Schools were established in the military camps and schoolmasters were sent out from England.

Recreation was not forgotten. Games of chess, dominoes, footballs, magic lanterns, and stereoscopes were sent to the soldiers. And Florence opened up a social center, the *Inkerman Coffee House,* named after one of the famous battle grounds of the Crimea. Here the soldiers could spend their free time without gambling and getting drunk—and a gratifying number of them did.

Until the Government took it over, Florence maintained a money order office. Here she received the money of any soldier who wished to send some portion of his pay home. Soon Flo was sending out large sums of money—1,000 pounds sterling, about $5,000—a month. Any soldier who promised *her* that he would send money home *did*. And any soldier who promised *her* he would not drink *didn't*.

Still uppermost in Florence's mind, however, was a return to the Crimea. There the hospital kitchens so carefully planned by Mr. Soyer remained unbuilt. There too the lack of discipline among the nurses was undermining the program. But Dr. Hall was as hostile as ever, insisting that her authority lay in Turkey, not in the Crimea.

In late July, the Bracebridges decided to return to England. They had served Florence faithfully for nine months. Perhaps now they could help her cause better at home.

Flo's family was worried at her being left "alone" so soon after her illness. And so, in September, her Aunt Mai arrived to take the place of Selina Bracebridge.

Aunt Mai was shocked to see her niece so worn, so thin, so pale. She resolved to keep Flo from working so hard.

But even Aunt Mai was not able to do that. Flo was not only doing the long hours of nursing, she was also keeping up with her enormously increased office work. The stream of people outside her door was longer than ever. She had a much larger nursing staff to direct. (By the time the war ended, she who had been concerned over managing forty nurses had one hundred and twenty-five under her control.)

Aunt Mai helped Flo by copying letters, reports, records. She attended to all the odd jobs Selina had done for Flo. She rose at five and fell into bed at eleven. But Flo, she told the family at home, "writes till one or two, sometimes till three or four."

Flo had a great deal to write about, much to arrange, in the time left to her in the East. A determined attack on

Sevastopol had finally routed the Russians and the seaport was taken in September, 1855. The Crimean War was over— or would be as soon as the treaty of peace was signed. But that could take many months, and Florence knew *her* work was far from finished.

The sick and wounded still had to be tended properly. It was also important to get her whole nursing staff to work together smoothly. At this last stage, neither the nursing nor the nurses must be allowed to fall apart, regardless of all the unpleasant personal battles she must wage. Her mission *must* end as a success. If only the War Office would confirm her position so that she would not have to fight stubborn officials every inch of the way. . . .

In November, when her situation in the Crimea was at its worst, in England her fame as a national heroine was at its height. She was becoming a legend. Returning soldiers sang her praises. Grateful families blessed her in their prayers. The news of her illness, and then of her recovery, and her resolve to remain at her post until the last soldier had embarked for home, elevated her almost to sainthood. People wanted to honor her in every way.

Some of these "honors" were sentimental "biographies," largely drawn from the writers' imaginations. Reams of poetry, good and bad, were written about her, and sometimes set to music. China statuettes, supposedly of Miss Nightingale, appeared in the shops. There were no portraits of her available, but that did not stop ambitious artists from inventing a "likeness" and selling it.

Streets were named for Florence, ships, a lifeboat—even an English racehorse!

Thousands of baby girls all over the world were named Florence, sometimes with Nightingale as the middle name. Strangers called on the Nightingales, asking to see something of hers, or to gaze at the place where *she* had lived, or even just to look at the family of the popular heroine.

Some of her loyal friends at home decided that she might appreciate another kind of tribute, one that would further her work. Vast sums of money were raised "for the training of nurses." And so the Nightingale Fund was born.

When word of the fund reached the soldiers, they responded by contributing nearly 9,000 pounds—close to $45,-000.

Queen Victoria wished to add a personal tribute to Miss Nightingale, to "mark her warm feelings of admiration." Her token was a brooch designed by Prince Albert especially for Miss Nightingale. This jeweled badge was in the form of a St. George's Cross in red enamel, surmounted by a diamond crown, with the Queen's royal initials, also in diamonds, below. At the foot of the cross was the word "Crimea," and encircling the cross, the words, "Blessed are the merciful." On the back of the brooch, the inscription: "To Miss Florence Nightingale, as a mark of esteem and gratitude for her devotion towards the Queen's brave soldiers from Victoria R. 1855."

With this handsome decoration came a personal letter from the Queen, written at Windsor Castle, praising Florence for her services in "this great and bloody war . . . services which are fully equal to those of my brave soldiers, whose sufferings you have had the *privilege* of alleviating in so merciful a manner. . . . It will be a very great satisfaction to me, when you return at last to these shores, to make the acquaintance of one who has set so bright an example to our sex."

Deeply touched though Florence was by all this, she wrote Sidney Herbert that the establishment of the training school for nurses would have to wait.

And so this large sum of money was put into a bank, while Miss Nightingale fought death and disease—and Dr. Hall.

Florence was able to return to the Crimea early in October. She was not welcomed.

"There is not an official who would not burn me like Joan of Arc if he could," she wrote Sidney Herbert. "But they know the War Office cannot turn me out because the country is with me."

In the Crimea some of Florence's efforts were bearing fruit. Mr. Soyer's diet kitchens were built and were now feeding hundreds of men. The hospitals were cleaner, and the nursing staffs were more efficient.

Then, to her dismay, she was recalled to Scutari in November. A new epidemic had broken out. She left with a heavy heart. So much was still undone in the Crimea. What would happen now in her absence?

Return of the Heroine

THE ROOT of her problem in the Crimea lay, Florence knew, in the original wording of her appointment: "Superintendent of the Female Nursing Establishment . . . *in Turkey.*" Despite her many requests, the War Office had still done nothing to clarify her official position. Now, unknown to Florence, influential people in England were working on her behalf. At long last Lord Panmure, Secretary of State for War, was stirred into action.

On March 16, a special dispatch from the War Office arrived in the Crimea. It was so important that the commander-in-chief was directed to publish it in the general orders of the day. This meant that the dispatch would be posted in every barrack and mess hall on the Crimea, and in Scutari, too. No one could possibly avoid reading the sharply worded message, or miss its full meaning.

"It appears to me," wrote Lord Panmure, "that the Medical Authorities of the Army do not correctly comprehend Miss Nightingale's position as it has been officially recognized by me. I therefore state briefly for their guidance, as well as for the information of the Army, what the position of that excellent lady is.

"Miss Nightingale is recognized by Her Majesty's Government as the General Superintendent of the Female Nursing Establishment of *the military hospitals of the Army*.

"No lady, or sister, or nurse, is to be transferred from one hospital to another, or introduced into any hospital without consultation with her. . . . The Principal Medical Officer will communicate with Miss Nightingale upon all subjects connected with the Female Nursing Establishment, and will give his directions through that lady."

The principal medical officer was Dr. Hall. The general order was thus a severe rebuke and a bitter blow to his stiff-necked pride.

For Florence it was a triumph. The struggle for the recognition of her mission was over. If only this authority had come sooner. . . .

It was not in Flo's nature, however, either to look back or to gloat. She arrived in Balaclava on March 24, in a blinding snowstorm, and was formally welcomed by the commander-in-chief. The next day she took her ten nurses to the Land Transport Hospital, where they were badly needed. And then she proceeded to work, as usual.

The peace treaty which officially ended the Crimean War was signed in Paris on March 30, 1856. On April 29 the good news was announced to the British Army and its allies. One by one, troop ships filled with soldiers sailed for home. One by one, the hospitals were emptied—and closed. The nurses, too, began to go home in small groups.

Miss Nightingale saw to it that every nurse was provided for. Those who qualified as professional hospital nurses were helped to find suitable positions in England. Many others she helped with her own money.

Florence returned to Scutari at the end of June, to an empty camp. On July 16, 1856, the last patient left the Barrack Hospital. Flo's work there was finished.

Yet she lingered.

Aunt Mai began their packing, casting anxious glances in Flo's direction. The Nightingale family was hoping that Flo would come home content. Surely she had done enough. Only that morning a letter had come from Mrs. Nightingale, asking, "When will you be coming home, Flo? We must know the exact time and place. Official receptions are being planned. . . ."

"Everyone is anxious to meet and talk with you, Flo," wrote Parthe. "You can't imagine how popular you are!"

Florence shrank from public acclaim. The idea of being treated as a national heroine distressed her greatly. Often Aunt Mai would waken in the night to find Flo pacing restlessly.

On one of those sleepless nights her aunt asked, "What is it Flo? What's wrong?"

Florence continued to pace back and forth in the pale light of a flickering lamp. She pulled a heavy wrapper about her, shivering, although the air was warm. Then she gazed beyond the windows toward the huge military cemetery where 8,000 British soldiers lay. "Wrong?" she repeated, and tears filled her eyes.

"It's over, dearest," her aunt comforted her. "There is nothing you can do to help them now. Come to bed. You must sleep."

"I can't sleep," Florence replied. "Every time I close my eyes I see them. Most of them died needlessly, so needlessly. They did not die of their wounds, Aunt Mai. The war did not kill them."

"What then, Flo?" Aunt Mai's uneasiness was growing.

"Neglect. Indifference. Stupidity. Unsanitary conditions. Inefficiency. Red tape. Lack of proper care." Florence covered her face with her thin white hands. "I see them now. The rows of beds, the horrible suffering. *I can never forget them!*"

It soon became apparent that Florence Nightingale did not intend to rest until she found some way to prevent such a disaster from ever happening again. *She would work to change the organization of army hospitals.* She would fight until she fulfilled what she now believed to be her secret promise to the valiant soldiers she had nursed.

Aunt Mai sighed when she heard of this new task Flo set herself. She saw that her niece had no intention of returning to England to become a dutiful daughter once more. Aunt Mai tried to tell the Nightingales this as tactfully as possible. Mrs. Nightingale ignored what she considered to be nonsense and continued her plans for social reception. After all, her daughter was the most famous and popular woman in England! The entire nation was prepared to honor her. There would be parades, bands, speeches, balls—and she and Parthe would be there, a part of it all!

The Government did indeed want to bring Florence back in state, aboard a battleship. She declined this honor. Where then would Miss Nightingale first set foot on British soil? Everyone wanted to know.

"The whole regiments of the Coldstreams, the Grenadiers and the Fusiliers would like to meet Flo," Parthe wrote ecstatically to Aunt Mai. "And failing that, they would like to send their bands to play her home wherever she might arrive, day or night."

No one was told where Florence Nightingale would land in England, or when. Not even her family knew.

Florence and Aunt Mai left Constantinople on July 28, 1856. A Queen's messenger went with them to attend to such details as their passports and baggage. This much Florence had agreed to. Then she and Aunt Mai embarked for the French port of Marseilles, as Mrs. and Miss Smith. In France, Florence spent a day and a half in Paris, with old friends. Aunt Mai continued on to England.

Thus Florence sailed from France to England alone. The

first thing she did when she set foot in England was to fulfill a promise she had made to the nuns in Scutari. "If I live to return to England, I shall come to you before I see anyone else," she had said.

At eight in the morning she rang the bell at the Convent of the Sisters of Mercy in Bermondsey. She stayed with the nuns for a few hours, and in the afternoon took a train north—still alone, still unrecognized.

Early in the evening of August 7, 1856, she stepped off the train at the little country station near Lea Hurst, and walked up the steep slope to the manor house.

Mrs. Watson, the housekeeper, adjusting a drape at the front window, saw a lady in a black traveling costume, carrying a small carpetbag, walk slowly up the driveway. Mrs. Watson looked more closely. *"It's Miss Florence!"* she shrieked, and she rushed out to welcome the nation's heroine, home from the war.

Parthe and her parents were only a step behind.

Laughing and crying, Flo embraced them all. "Everything is exactly as I remembered it," she said. She gazed at the wide lawns and gardens, and the high, misty hills beyond. "Best of all," she said to her family, "you are the same."

At this Parthe's tears flowed. *They* had not changed in two years. But Flo looked years older—thin, drawn, and weary, and much, much sadder, even in the gladness of homecoming.

The next day, the peal of the small church bell on the hills, and a thanksgiving prayer at the little chapel, welcomed Florence Nightingale home. No bands. No shouting and cheering, or speechmaking. It was all the greeting she wanted.

Florence Nightingale's family fondly hoped that her work was finished, that her reputation and her fame would now content her. They did not understand at all that she cared nothing about her fame and that in her reputation she saw only an opportunity for further work.

But for the present, Florence needed rest—and Lea Hurst was the ideal place for this. How often she had thought of her hilltop home, remembering the sound of the Derwent River rushing along its deep valley of red and misty-purple rocks. She lay on her sofa listening to it now, her eyes closed. Now the sound recalled to her the roar of the Bosporus.

She moved restlessly, and at once her mother adjusted the shawl spread over her feet. "Rest . . ." she told her daughter.

"Rest . . ." Parthe kept saying.

"Rest, Miss Florence, rest," Mrs. Watson the housekeeper murmured each time she came in to straighten up the room.

"Nourishing food and rest—complete rest—are necessary to regain your health," the doctors said. It was an endless chorus.

But Florence could neither eat nor rest. She could not empty her mind of the thoughts and plans that churned inside her head. Day after day she lay on the sofa, physically exhausted. At times she found it difficult to breathe. She had fainting spells and the sight of food made her ill. Yet at night she found the strength to pace the floor of her room, and the sound of the rushing Derwent then was like thunder in her ears.

Florence Nightingale knew that everything she had done in the Crimea would be wasted unless army hospitals—and indeed, the whole approach to the health and welfare of the soldiers—were reorganized and reformed. Unless the British War Office learned from the terrible fact that 73 per cent of their men had died of neglect in six months, it could happen again. The men Florence had watched die needlessly would have died in vain. She *must* find a way to have her ideas accepted.

She was faced with two difficulties. She was a woman,

and she was a national heroine. She still faced the jealousy of powerful medical men, who felt she had diminished *their* glory. They would oppose anything she proposed. And Florence knew only too well that it was the *men* who made the important decisions in government.

"If I could only find a spokesman," Flo thought, "an influential man to speak for me!"

She wrote to Lord Panmure, the Secretary of State for War. But he was evasive. "It is more important for you to rest now," he told her.

Then she wrote to Sidney Herbert. Because he was genuinely concerned about her health, he too answered, "Follow the advice of the doctors—don't read, don't write, don't even think."

Florence refused to be put off. In August, 1856, she wrote in her private notes, "I stand at the altar of the murdered men and while I live, I fight their cause."

At last, in September, she received some real encouragement. Sir James Clark, an old friend—and physician to the Queen—invited her to visit his estate Birk Hall, in the Scottish Highlands. He wrote at the Queen's suggestion, he told Florence. Her Majesty was at Balmoral Castle—only two miles away. The Queen wished to hear of Miss Nightingale's experiences in the East.

Instantly Flo's ills were forgotten. She rose from her sofa. Quickly all her notes and figures and facts were organized, bags packed, good-byes said, and—accompanied by her father —she left for Birk Hall in Scotland, her spirits high.

The Nightingale's Magic Power

FLORENCE NIGHTINGALE was asked to visit Balmoral Castle on the afternoon of September 21. That day, as she was driven to the castle, she recalled her first meeting with the Queen. Florence had been nineteen when she was presented to the equally young Victoria. Now both of them were mature women, and they had something more in common. The Queen knew what it meant to be a woman in a man's world. She had the royal title, Victoria Regina, but little direct power.

Under British law the Queen could not issue orders of national importance and have them obeyed. Whatever she wanted done by the Government had to come through her ministers and Parliament. But the Queen *could* and *did* use her great influence. Remembering this, Florence relaxed against the cushions of the carriage. She could depend on the Queen.

Florence Nightingale's meeting with Queen Victoria and Albert, the Prince Consort, was an informal one. They talked for more than two hours. The royal pair were charmed with Florence, and deeply moved by her selfless dedication.

That night the Prince wrote in his journal: "She put before us all the defects of our present military system and the reforms that are needed. We are much pleased with her; and she is extremely modest."

Queen Victoria marveled over Flo's genius for organization. "What a clear head!" Her Majesty exclaimed. "I wish we had her at the War Office."

Florence was invited to Balmoral Castle again and again. She went to church with the royal family, and she dined with them informally on several occasions. One afternoon the servants at Birk Hall were astonished to see the Queen drive herself to the manor in a pony cart. She alighted, nodded graciously to the butler and the footmen who bowed low before her, and asked for Miss Nightingale.

That day she took Florence for a long walk.

There were other visits. Sometimes Queen Victoria spent the whole afternoon with Florence and stayed for tea. She was enchanted with Miss Nightingale and ready to help her cause. By the end of September, Queen Victoria and Miss Nightingale had formed a plan of action.

"You will have to convince Lord Panmure of the necessity for army reform." Queen Victoria warned. "Only he can give an investigating committee official standing. And our Secretary of State for War is a very difficult man."

Florence smiled. "I've dealt with difficult men before. Most of them can be managed."

There was an amused twinkle in the Queen's eyes. "So you have learned that lesson, too," she said.

Her Majesty arranged a meeting between Florence Nightingale and Lord Panmure at Balmoral Castle on October 5, 1856.

A timid person would have been overwhelmed by Lord Panmure's appearance. He was a big man, with a very large head and an enormous amount of hair. He had a way of shaking his head from side to side, and he was known to be stubborn. At the War Office he had been nicknamed "the Bison." It was such a suitable name that Florence had to suppress a smile at their first meeting.

Lord Panmure's sharp eyes seemed to bore through Florence, as if trying to discover just what she wanted for herself. So many people came to him with selfish requests. "The Queen has forwarded to me an outline for army reform," he told her crisply. "*Your* outline, I believe. What more can you tell me about it?"

The burly Scot had come to scoff at Florence Nightingale's ideas. He left under the spell of her charm and intelligence.

With Lord Panmure's approval, a royal commission to investigate the reform of army hospitals was organized by January, 1857.

The commission was made up of both military and civilian doctors. Sidney Herbert agreed to act as chairman. He was to be Florence's spokesman, and conduct the public business which she as a woman could not carry on. Florence could have wished for no better man to champion the cause of reform. Mr. Herbert was tactful and wise in dealing with difficult people.

It was important now for Florence to be present in London. She took rooms at the Burlington Hotel with her mother and Parthe. There, while Mama and Parthe happily entertained their guests in the drawing room, Florence and the committee met daily in the small adjoining sitting room. The men called Flo's sitting room the "little war office," and they referred to her as the "commander-in-chief."

The work was exacting, satisfying—and exhausting. Florence had to inspect hospitals and barracks, conduct interviews at distant points, then return home and write out her long reports. She traveled by hansom cab when she could get one; by public horse-drawn bus when she could not, by train when necessary. It never occurred to her mother or Parthe to place their carriage at Flo's disposal. No one on her committee thought of it either. Sometimes she had to walk miles through wind and rain, and then miles more along hospital corridors to get the facts for her reports.

Neither Mrs. Nightingale nor Parthe had any idea of the importance of Flo's "new interest." They spoke of her tenderly, they wrote about her in fine phrases—but still understood her not at all. At night, when she returned exhausted, they scolded her for not going to parties. It was all too bitterly clear. They had not changed, Florence thought wearily. But she had.

She no longer craved their sympathy and understanding. Only her work was important now. She had never fully recovered from her Crimean exhaustion, and it seemed to her that she never would. Still, she drove herself and the committee hard.

Dr. Sutherland, a sanitation expert who had been at Scutari and Balaclava, said of her, "She is the mainspring of the work. Nobody who has not worked with her daily could know her, could have an idea of her strength and clearness of mind, her extraordinary powers and goodness of spirit. She is one of the most gifted creatures God ever made."

Under Flo's tireless, fiery leadership, the commission was soon ready to submit its reports to Parliament. If there were no more delays, the reforms proposed by the commission would soon become laws. British soldiers would never again lack food, clothing, and medical attention and be helpless victims of neglect in poorly run hospitals.

At this point Lord Panmure began to hesitate. The commission's report criticized many officials. He was worried about public opinion. He was worried about the reaction of the army medical officers. He worried about retaining his position as Secretary of State for War. He refused to act.

Florence met him privately. Lord Panmure was stubborn. She saw that more than truth and charm were needed now.

"Do I understand that you refuse to make the work of our commission official?" she asked him icily.

"My dear Miss Nightingale, it is not a matter of refusal." Lord Panmure threw up his hands.

"What, then?" she probed.

"It is a matter of politics. One must move cautiously."

Florence's clear gray eyes narrowed. "Cautiously—or not at all?" she asked.

The Bison swayed his head from side to side uncomfortably. "It is difficult for a woman to understand politics," he hedged.

"Not as difficult as you think," Miss Nightingale retorted. "Politics is often a matter of public opinion, is it not?"

The Bison nodded.

"Then consider this, sir. If you do not act officially *at once,* I shall publish the complete story of my work at the Barrack Hospital. I shall tell of the neglect, the hopeless confusion, and the unspeakable suffering. What will the effect of public opinion be then?"

Within a month the work of the royal commission was made official. This led to the great changes that were eventually made in the care of the English soldiers. As a result of the commission's work, military and medical organizations throughout the world were able to correct unsanitary and inhumane conditions that had been accepted as inevitable until the brilliant work of Florence Nightingale brought enlightenment.

Florence Nightingale was victorious—but once more at the price of her health. In August of 1857, Flo collapsed so completely that even she admitted that she was ill. However, she violently refused to be nursed by her family.

"I will go to Malvern," she declared. This was a quiet village in western England, where people went for rest cures.

Parthe offered to go with her, but Flo refused. "I must go alone. I must *be* alone," she insisted. "I have not been alone for four years." Her sudden vehemence frightened Parthe into silence.

Florence was sent off by train, in an invalid carriage. A family manservant was given instructions to deliver her to the doctors at a Malvern retreat. She would have it no other way.

When her father visited her at Malvern, he was appalled. Florence appeared to be dying. It was unthinkable that someone from the family should not be with her. Aunt Mai was called, and once again she left her husband and family and rushed to Florence. Aunt Mai never irritated her and never misunderstood her, and Flo responded to her presence.

The stay at Malvern helped her, but this collapse marked the beginning of Florence Nightingale's life as an invalid.

In September she returned to London and took rooms of her own at the Burlington Hotel. Aunt Mai came to look after her—and to guard her against visitors, "like a dragon," Parthe declared. Even she and her mother were asked not to call. Only Mr. Nightingale was allowed to slip in to see Flo. "I shall always be well enough to see *you*," Flo had written him. Selina Bracebridge too was allowed to come, but other visitors were screened carefully by Aunt Mai and Dr. Sutherland. Every ounce of Flo's strength must be carefully guarded.

The doctors agreed that Florence did not have any specific disease. She was suffering from the exhaustion of almost every nerve and organ in her body. They said her health would never improve, and only constant care and rest could prolong her life.

But Florence could not rest unless she worked. For her life had no meaning without her work. Whenever guidance was needed, she continued to give it. Most recently she had become concerned about the living conditions of the British Army in India, and of the Indian people who lived under British rule. Important officials were begging for appointments with her.

She did see them, one at a time. While these people were with her, they had her fullest attention. She talked with them so briskly and brilliantly, they had no idea of her physical weakness. Afterward, she often fainted. Indeed, her life seemed to hang by a thread and she, herself, expected to die soon. But she intended to accomplish as much as possible while there was breath in her body.

Her family was more than ever alarmed, especially when Florence asked Uncle Sam Smith to help her make her will. There was the Nightingale Fund to consider . . . and in a letter to Parthe she expressed her wish to be buried in the Crimea, among the soldiers she had nursed.

Yet Florence never allowed her work to slacken. Also, she was now writing two books—one on hospitals, and the other on nursing. Somehow she managed to write hundreds of pages of closely written notes, as well as hundreds of pages of reports and suggestions to be used by her various committees.

For two years Florence scarcely left her bedroom. Whenever her condition seemed worse than usual, she was taken from London to Malvern in an invalid carriage. Refreshed by a week's rest, she would return to the Burlington and the rooms she had made bright and cheerful. The faithful workers in Flo's "little war office" were frequently invited for special breakfasts, lunches, and dinners, which were followed by business talks.

During the summer of 1857, Flo had met a handsome widower, Sir Harry Verney. He had admired her work for a long time. Now he became a frequent visitor. He was a Member of Parliament, and had supported the reforms Florence worked so hard to put through. Sir Harry fell in love with Florence and asked her to marry him.

Flo had given up all thought of marriage years ago, when she had refused to marry Richard Monckton Milnes. She admired Sir Harry and enjoyed his company—but her work, she explained as gently as she could, still came first. Sir Harry remained her lifelong friend and supporter.

That winter the lonely widower visited the Nightingales at Embley. Eventually he proposed marriage to Parthe, and she accepted. Mrs. Nightingale was delighted. It was an excellent match even though Sir Harry was much older than Parthe and had four grown children. He was noble and kind, and very rich. The excitement of preparing for a wedding pleased Mrs. Nightingale enormously, and the prospect of becoming Lady Verney occupied Parthe completely. The wedding took place at Embley in June of 1858.

The pressure of her family's social bustle was lifted from Florence. Now Parthe had her own home to manage—Claydon House—and Mama had another place to visit. Florence could go on with her work and her writing in peace.

In 1859 Florence published her book *Notes on Hospitals*. It was an immediate success, and its influence was worldwide. For the next fifty years few hospitals were built without consultation of this book, or Miss Nightingale herself. The Queen of Holland and the Crown Princess of Prussia patiently waited their turn for an appointment with Miss Nightingale. Dukes, ministers, and lords called upon her. The King of Portugal asked her to design a hospital for Lisbon, and her plans were accepted.

All this required vast correspondence and endless hours of toil from a woman who could scarcely rise from her couch. And yet, some months later, in December of 1859, Florence published another book: *Notes on Nursing*.

The Queen's physician, Sir James Clark, said that this

book would do more to promote good health in the home than anything that had ever been written.

In the introduction to this slim little book for the general public, Miss Nightingale stated that her Notes were not intended to teach nurses to nurse. "They are meant simply to give hints for thought to women who have personal charge of the health of others. Every woman . . . has, at one time or another of her life, charge of the personal health of somebody, whether child or invalid—in other words, every woman is a nurse."

This book was an immediate popular success—not only because it was full of practical wisdom, but also because this was the first public word from the Lady with the Lamp since her return from the Crimea. People had no idea of what Miss Nightingale had been doing. It was known that she had gone into retirement. But it was *not* known that the recent upheavals in the War Office and the various army reforms had come through her. Her work behind the scenes of the Government was always a closely guarded secret.

Now people flocked to buy copies of her *Notes on Nursing*, especially when it was found that here and there she recalled her experiences in the Crimean War. The tone of her writing was gentle, witty, womanly. She was as concerned with preserving family health through cleanliness, good ventilation, and good sanitary conditions as she was with giving sensible directions for the treatment of the sick.

One result of reading the book was that people who had feared "the bad night air" began to sleep with their windows open, because Miss Nightingale advised it!

Before the end of the first month, 15,000 copies were sold. Soon *Notes on Nursing* was distributed in factories, villages, and schools. Everyone seemed to be reading it. The small seventy-page book was published in many other countries and translated into German, French, and Italian. It was immediately printed in the United States, and reprinted many times. Even today copies can be found in local libraries and in the medical libraries of our universities. The material is fresh and gay—as well as serious—and much of it just as useful as the day it was first published.

The tremendous public response to the book once more called attention to the vast Nightingale Fund, collected to help Florence establish a training school for nurses. People wanted to see this fund put to use.

Florence Nightingale had never lost her concern for nurses and nursing, but the work for hospital and army reforms had pushed it aside temporarily. Now, once again, plans to found a school of nursing were discussed with her.

Aunt Mai was certain that her niece could not stand the strain of such a project. The members of the committee for the Nightingale Fund were equally certain that no one but Miss Nightingale could carry through this difficult project successfully.

Dismayed, Aunt Mai urged Flo to turn the work over to someone else. "It is less than four years since you returned from the Crimea," she protested. "Yet you have already done enough for several lifetimes."

"But this is something I must do," Florence said, propped up in bed among her cushions. Her eyes grew bright with hope for fulfillment of her lifelong dream—the long-awaited training school which would raise the position of nurses to the ranks of respected professionals.

The Nightingale School

WHERE to establish the Nightingale Training School? This was the first problem to be solved.

There were many good reasons for deciding on the old St. Thomas's Hospital, near London Bridge. It was large and well managed. More important, the hospital was soon to have a new building in another part of town. Florence would have much to say about its design and equipment.

"When we rebuild," Florence told her co-workers, "we will add a house for our nurses. Meanwhile, the hospital has offered us a wing of the present building for our school. Really, the situation couldn't be better."

Her enthusiasm set her to working sixteen hours a day on her plans to equip and set up the training schedule for the "Nightingales." There was no possibility that Florence could take charge of the school in person. She could leave her couch only for short periods, and could scarcely stand alone. So finding the right superintendent for the student nurses of the Nightingale Training School was of utmost importance. And here again she was in luck. When Florence interviewed the matron of St. Thomas's Hospital, she found her to be exactly the sort of person her school required.

Mrs. Wardroper was a small and energetic lady of immense dignity and indisputable authority. At forty-two she had been left a widow with four young children. Rather than become a genteel poor relation in the family, Mrs. Wardroper struck out independently and became a nurse. It was an attitude and a situation Florence could understand.

"I don't suppose your relatives approved of your decision," she remarked dryly.

Mrs. Wardroper had led a hard life, but it had not spoiled her sense of humor. She smiled. "You might put it that way. But it was something I wanted to do—in fact, *had* to do—and with no school to teach me."

The words were familiar.

Florence liked the matron's belief in discipline and her high ideals for the nursing profession. Together they would make the Nightingale Training School a success.

Although Mrs. Wardroper was enthusiastic, she was also realistic. "We must be prepared for harsh criticism," she told Florence.

"I have never been seriously wounded by criticism," Florence said lightly.

"Some will come from within the hospital itself," the matron pointed out. "You are, of course, familiar with Dr. South's views."

Florence certainly was. The senior surgeon of St. Thomas's had written some *Observations on Training Establishments for Hospitals.* He felt they were entirely unnecessary for "ward-maids." Nurses, he said, learned by experience and they needed only the simplest instructions on how to make poultices and beds. They were, after all, in the same position as housemaids.

"We shall just have to prove Dr. South, and those who think like him, quite wrong," Florence declared.

In May of 1860, the first advertisements for applicants to the Nightingale Training School appeared in the newspapers. Fifteen young women were selected to begin training on July 9, 1860.

Every detail of their schooling, conduct, and housing had been carefully thought out. For the first time there was such a thing as a nurses' home. Each of the probationers, or "probies," as the student nurses were called, had a bedroom of her own. There was also a sitting room to be shared by all. Florence had provided this with books, pictures, and vases. She planned to have flowers sent down regularly from Embley. Unable to leave her bed, Florence depended on trusted friends to see that her wishes were carried out.

Escorted by Mrs. Wardroper, Selina Bracebridge made a tour of inspection of the nurses' home on an upper floor of St. Thomas's Hospital. She viewed the nurses' quarters with considerable interest—and perhaps with vivid recollections of the dismal nurses' tower in Scutari.

"This is so attractive and comfortable," Selina said.

Mrs. Wardroper agreed, but appeared doubtful about the "extras" insisted on by Miss Nightingale. "I feel we may spoil the girls with such comforts," she said. "They cannot expect all this when they leave us for actual hospital positions."

Florence had no intention of spoiling her young nurses, but she believed that pleasant surroundings were an aid to well-being. Her new "daughters" were not to scrub and scour and waste their energy in being housemaids. But she expected them to work hard.

The girls were required to rise at six, work all day long, and at night to write up their notes for the day. They washed patients, made beds, assisted the ward nurses, and received instruction from the most experienced sisters, as head nurses were called in England. The probies were required to serve meals to the patients and feed those who needed help. For their own meals they were allowed half an hour, with fifteen minutes for getting to and from the dining hall.

When the house physicians arrived, the probies were divided into small groups and made the rounds with them as they examined the patients. They had to observe each patient carefully and write out reports on each one. With the surgeons, they were taught to change dressings, and told about the special care of surgical patients.

In the afternoons visiting doctors gave lectures on anatomy, diseases and their effect on the body, and on many other subjects that Florence had longed so vainly to learn when she was a girl.

The probationers did have short periods of rest during the day. And there was tea at five, which revived them somewhat and kept them going until about nine at night. By that time all the patients were ready for the night.

Back in their rooms, the probies would dearly have loved to collapse on their beds. But one more duty awaited them—

the notes required of them by Miss Nightingale and Mrs. Wardroper.

When the probationers had time to relax in their sitting room, they often talked about the problem of meeting Miss Nightingale's standards.

"Notes on everything—just everything! Every tiny detail," complained one dark-haired girl. "I don't know if I can get it all down. I have never done so much writing in my whole life!"

"Nevertheless, you had better try," advised a more serious-minded probie. "Be especially careful to keep everything up-to-date. Mrs. Wardroper said she might call for our notebooks at any time. She meant it!"

"Oh, glory!" cried the first girl. "Do you think Miss Nightingale will see them, too?"

"I wouldn't doubt it. She read our last examination papers. She manages to keep an eye on everything we do."

"Oooooh!" the little probie wailed and glanced around as if she half expected to see eyes staring at her from the walls. And then she fled to her room and her notebook.

A tall, pretty girl, looking out of the window, called to the others in the sitting room. They all watched as two probationers left by the front door of the hospital. The girls walked close together, sedately following the hospital rule that no probationer was ever to go out alone. But as they reached the corner, the girls separated and shot off in different directions.

Everyone in the sitting room laughed. This was something they all did when they had time off—always hoping their sin of separation would not be observed by Mrs. Wardroper.

The strict rules were necessary for these high-spirited young women who were pioneers in *trained* nursing. It was the word "trained" that was destined to make a world of difference in the public image of the hospital nurse. Meanwhile, people in London were following with interest the progress of the Nightingale probationers. Some of the medical men were certain that women could never learn anything useful about anatomy and disease. The whole newfangled business of "training" was sheer nonsense, they proclaimed loudly. Accustomed to the common, tipsy slatterns of that period, they simply would not believe that Miss Nightingale's methods could produce intelligent nurses of the highest character, ideals, and trained skill.

Florence was equally convinced that she could do just that. She believed there were two ways to accomplish it: first, by careful selection of probationers, and second, by rigid enforcement of the school rules.

A constant check was kept on each girl. The matron sent Florence detailed monthly reports. In addition, Mrs. Wardroper wrote long, confidential, personal reports on the student nurses.

For all the strict discipline, the probationers led a pleasant life. They worked hard, but they learned much. They were ladylike and neat. It was becoming increasingly clear that the Nightingale Nurses were vastly different from the slovenly women who staffed the ordinary hospitals. These girls wore a uniform—something taken for granted today, but an innovation then. They wore a brown dress and snowy white caps and aprons. A magazine writer said they "looked like bits of extra light as they moved cheerfully and noiselessly from bed to bed."

This favorable description received much attention. Mrs. Wardroper began to get requests for Nightingale Nurses from many parts of the country. When the first class graduated at the end of the year, a wide choice of positions was open to the girls. Thirteen of the original fifteen probies received their certificates. Six of these stayed on at St. Thomas's Hospital.

As probationers they had been supplied with room, board, laundry, and uniforms by the Nightingale Fund. They were also given about fifty dollars in spending money during their one year of training. Those who worked in hospitals for a year after becoming certificated nurses received an additional sum of money. Florence Nightingale expected her nurses to continue in hospital work and, by their example, to help reform poor conditions wherever they went. In time, she hoped that her girls would become teachers and even superintendents in other training schools. Her trained girls were meant to be leaders, and most of the Nightingales did not disappoint her.

At the end of the first year, the school was judged a tremendous success. Now there were more applicants than could be handled. Florence began to look forward to the time when the school would be enlarged in the hospital's new quarters.

But the bright triumphant summer turned suddenly dark for Flo. On August 2, 1861, her dear friend Sidney Herbert died.

Everything she had accomplished had been done with his aid. Now, without him, Florence felt lost. She did not know whether she could continue to work at all.

It was the Civil War in America that brought Florence out of her grief. The war had been declared in April, 1861. In October, President Lincoln's Secretary of War appealed to Florence for help in organizing hospitals for the American soldiers. The conditions described reminded Florence of the sickening disorder and misery she had found in Scutari. Once again she saw before her row upon row of desperately sick and wounded men. She relived the horror of death through neglect. And once again Florence Nightingale was moved to action.

A Woman's Central Association of Relief had been formed

in New York, she learned. Female nurses were being allowed to enter the Northern military hospitals, because Florence Nightingale had proved it could be done. But now those volunteers needed help—advice on such matters as proper diet and cooking techniques.

Soon Flo's pen was flying across the pages, this time for the benefit of the United States.

The Nightingale Nurses

THE BUILDING of the new St. Thomas's Hospital occupied much of Florence Nightingale's attention for several years. Even though she could not watch over the work personally, she was consulted about every detail of its construction and equipment.

By October of 1865 she was settled in a home of her own, at No. 10 South Street, in Mayfair, near the center of London. She lived here for forty-five years and it was from this house that she continued, as she called it, to "arrange things" for the rest of her long and remarkable life. Here she became *the* authority on special problems and Indian matters for the British Government. Engineers, supply officers, medical men— everyone concerned with that far corner of the British Empire wrote to her for advice. It became the custom for every newly appointed Viceroy of India to pay a visit to Miss Nightingale before leaving England.

At the same time, she continued to use her influence for reform in laws to help the poor, improve conditions in workhouses and insane asylums, and to change laws concerned with the right of women to own property. On all these matters she could always quote facts and figures to prove that reforms were necessary. Her friends said that Flo read such facts the way other people read novels.

Her vast knowledge made her a force to contend with. But how much or how little she was able to influence the Government depended on politics—on who was in office, and on which men in the Cabinet were in favor of reform. When the forward-looking men were out of office, Florence felt that *she* was "out of office" too, for then her influence was greatly lessened and she was quite discouraged. At such times she felt most keenly, though she still worked ten to sixteen hours a day, that she was not doing enough.

It was during one such period of gloom that a friend whom she greatly respected wrote her, ". . . you work on in silence, and nobody knows how many lives are saved by your nurses in hospitals (you have introduced a new era in nursing): how many thousand soldiers are now alive . . . owing to your forethought and diligence . . . how many natives of India (they might be counted probably by hundreds of thousands) have been preserved by the energy of a sick Lady who can scarcely rise from her bed. . . . But I know it and often think about it, and I want you to, so that in later years . . . you may see what a blessed life yours is and has been. . . ."

In 1871 the new St. Thomas's Hospital was at last completed. Queen Victoria herself opened the hospital on a bright June day, and the Nightingale Training School was moved into its new quarters.

The excellent Mrs. Wardroper remained its superintendent —a post she held for twenty-seven years—but Flo became the active head of the school and the chief of the Nightingale Nurses.

With the school so much larger now, Florence engaged an assistant superintendent, called the "home sister." This lady encouraged the students to read and study, to listen to music, and to go to church. The Nightingale Nurses were to be well-rounded, educated women.

Because they were to be trained to train others, they were also encouraged to be more patient and tactful. Florence had discovered that frequently her graduates, proud of their new, trained skills, considered *their* way of doing things the *only* way and the *best* way. Florence knew that this could only create antagonism, not bring about reforms. Her nurses must obey existing authority, and follow the rules of the institutions to which they were sent. Conditions in many institutions were still dreadful, but the people in charge must come to believe in the new way, if real change was to take place.

It was hard to teach this to the impatient young pioneers in modern nursing, but the essential lesson had to be learned. In replying to a letter from one of her nurses, who had written in a moment of great discouragement, Florence recalled her own experiences and frustrations in Crimea: "Do you think," she asked, "I should have succeeded in doing anything if I had kicked and resisted and resented? . . . I have been shut out of hospitals into which I had been ordered by the Commander-in-Chief, obliged to stand outside the door in the snow until night, have been refused rations for as much as ten days at a time for the nurses I had brought by superior command. I have been as good friends the day after with the officials who did these things—have resolutely ignored these things *for the sake of the work*."

Miss Nightingale had made her point.

Florence became personally acquainted with every "probie" as soon as her trial period was completed. For the young nurse, this meant a visit and an interview with the lady-in-chief herself. Many a probie grew faint with fright at the prospect, but usually emerged from the encounter starry-eyed and determined to please Miss Nightingale in everything.

As soon as the door closed on a girl, Florence wrote a vivid character sketch of her.

"Miss C——. A most capable little person . . . seems as good as can be. No complaints . . . enthusiasm for her work . . . and for the Sisters. Likes the bustle and hard work of Surgical Ward. . . ."

Or, "Miss H——. Tituppy, flippant, pretension-y. . . . Ambitious, clever, not much feeling. Talk-y. . . ."

"Miss V——. More cleverness than judgement, more activity than order, more hard sense than feeling, never any high view of her calling, always thinking more of appearance than of the truth. . . ."

"Miss G——. A woman of good feeling and bad sense. . . . She wants a very steady hand over her. . . ."

Many of the young women Florence interviewed were of excellent character, but it was the defects she wished to search out and correct, if possible. Each girl's file contained the character sketch, along with results of examinations— letters and comments sent by the matron and the home sister. Florence invited the students to comment on their lectures and their work. If a just complaint or a good suggestion was made, Florence followed it up promptly.

Each nurse who graduated from the Nightingale training school was like a missionary who went forth to teach new ideas. Florence therefore carefully studied each girl's file so that her graduate nurses would be placed in posts where they would do the most good. Since she never lost track of any of her nurses, each file continued to grow through the years.

When one of her graduate nurses went to a new post, Florence saw to it that flowers and a fond letter were sent ahead to welcome her. If it was a long journey, someone was waiting at the train with a basket of lunch.

If a nurse became ill, she was sent special diet foods. If

she needed rest, or a change, she was sent to the country or the seaside at Miss Nightingale's expense.

A nurse or matron who was overworked might be invited to No. 10 South Street for "a Saturday to Monday in bed," with Flo's housekeeper to care for her needs.

In June of 1873 Florence wrote: "I am immersed in such a torrent of my trained matrons and nurses, going and coming, to and from Edinburgh and Dublin, to and from watering places for their health, dining, tea-ing, sleeping—sleeping by day as well as by night. . . ." But this was the kind of "immersion" Florence loved best. From it she drew new strength and energy for her school and for her "daughters," her nurses.

Gradually other schools were established, often under the direction of Miss Nightingale's ablest nurses. By 1880 most of the important nursing posts in England were filled by Nightingale Nurses. They were the matrons and the superintendents in the major hospitals and institutions not only in the British Isles, but also in Canada, the United States, Sweden, Germany, India, Ceylon, and Australia.

Wherever a Nightingale Nurse went, her lady-in-chief went with her, not only in spirit but in deed. She stood behind every one of her graduates, ready with encouragement, guidance, with spirit-lifting messages and heartwarming little gifts. "Should there be anything in which I can be of the least use, here I am," was the way she ended many of her letters.

The success of her school and of her nurses had a healing effect on Flo's body, too. Occasionally, her brother-in-law, Sir Harry Verney, was able to persuade her to go driving with him in the London parks. Now and then she was even able to stroll along the paths, leaning upon his strong arm.

These outings had to be kept a secret from the general public. The Lady with the Lamp was a beloved legend. Sometimes in theater crowds, or on the streets, some pale lady in black would be mistaken for Miss Nightingale. Immediately she would be surrounded by an excited crowd, with people begging to touch her hand or her shawl or her gown. Florence had no wish to run into anything of this sort.

The Nightingale Training School had been in existence for twenty-two years, but Florence had never actually seen it. On January 27, 1882, Florence Nightingale paid her first and only visit to the new St. Thomas's Hospital. She inspected the quarters of the training school and one of the hospital wards with immense satisfaction. It was all exactly as she had pictured it—as she had directed it to be. It took the usually calm Mrs. Wardroper a week to recover from the excitement of this historic visit.

Florence was satisfied with her school and the course of training for her nurses, but she knew that her girls must never stop learning.

Great discoveries were being made in medicine. Anesthetics were now commonly used to control pain; antiseptics were used to control infections; new kinds of surgery were now possible—and this was only a beginning. Florence foresaw even greater advances, and she also realized that nurses would have to keep pace with the progress made by the doctors.

In a talk which she prepared for her pupils, she said, "For us who nurse, our nursing is a thing in which, unless we are making *progress* every year, every month, every week— take my word for it, we are going *back*. The more experience we gain, the more progress we can make. The progress you make in your year's training with us is as nothing to what you must make every year *after* your year's training is over. A woman who thinks, 'Now I'm a full nurse, a skilled nurse, I have learned all that there is to be learned' does not know what a nurse is, and she will never know. She is gone back already."

The Nightingale Nurses called their chief's messages "trumpet calls to duty" and few remained unmoved by them.

In 1887 Queen Victoria celebrated her golden jubilee— fifty years on the throne of the British Empire. Privately, Florence considered this her jubilee year also. Fifty years before, in February of 1837, *she* had received a call to service, a call that she had answered to the best of her ability.

The Closing Years

FLORENCE NIGHTINGALE, who at one time had thought that
she would never see her fortieth birthday, outlived all of her
immediate family and her closest friends. Strangely, in old
age her health was better than it had been in her middle
years. On her seventy-fifth birthday, May 12, 1895, she
wrote, "I have lost much in failure and disappointments, as
well as in grief, but do you know, life is more precious to
me now. . . . Life is a splendid gift!"

She made the most of every moment, for "the last years
of life were and ought to be the best," she said. Secretly,
Florence feared a lonely and useless old age. And yet, year
after year, she was able to write happily to one friend or
another, "I have my hands full and am not idle . . . *I am
soaked* in work!"

This surge of physical vigor could not last. Gradually
Flo's strength ebbed, and after 1896 she never left her South
Street bedroom. Her mind remained clear and active as
ever and she kept up with everything that was going on.
Her interest in all her projects was as keen as ever.

She continued to carry on her voluminous correspondence

with her nurses, matrons, and superintendents at their far-flung posts. Important people from all over the world still sought her advice, and waited patiently on her doorstep for a chance to see her in person. Florence was nearing eighty—but she certainly was not alone, and she could scarcely feel useless!

A housekeeper now lived with Miss Nightingale and had charge of her house. One of her nurses was also engaged to care for her. This, Florence said, was nonsense—she did not need a nurse. Frequently, at night, after the nurse had tucked her in, Florence would get up and somehow find the strength to go to the nurse's bed and tuck her in!

Suggestions from Miss Nightingale's book *Notes on Nursing* were now used in her own care as an invalid. Pets, which she had said "helped to cheer a patient" now included six cats, all affectionately spoiled by their famous mistress. Many of her notes and letters bore mysterious little smudges, which on closer inspection proved to be cat-paw prints over fresh ink.

Young nieces, nephews, and cousins, in whose lives she had become involved as she grew older, were now welcome visitors. Aunt Mai's and Sir Harry's grandchildren were special favorites—and the present Sir Harry Verney said when he was fifteen that she was his "favorite and perfect Aunt." Florence was never too busy or too tired to listen to their problems, to exclaim over examination papers, or to listen to confessions of first love, or young heartbreak.

Her private life was still carefully guarded, and long before 1897 most people thought that the heroine of the Crimea was dead. Reports to that effect had circulated from time to time for years. But in 1897, at the diamond jubilee for Queen Victoria—to celebrate her sixty years on the throne —there was an exhibition to show the tremendous progress of nursing during the Victorian era. This was planned around

Florence Nightingale and her heroic pioneer work, and she was asked to provide some personal things for it. As usual, Florence was reluctant "to go on public display." Finally she allowed a portrait and a bust of herself to be shown. Then someone found her old Crimean carriage at Embley, and that was brought down, too, and of course her lamp.

Excitement ran high as people thronged to see these possessions of the lady who had become such a legend in her own lifetime. The old soldiers Florence had once nursed in the Crimea looked at her things as if they were sacred.

"Think of that! The Lady ain't dead!" they told one another as they went up to touch the carriage and gaze at the lamp. Someone brought fresh flowers every day and decorated Miss Nightingale's statue with them. When she heard of it, she said she didn't like any of this—*not at all.*

The true fruits of the Crimean War, she said, were the tremendous lessons learned from the tremendous blunders. And the beginning of trained nursing, which was made possible afterward.

For Florence, the occasion was one for giving thanks to God, for "the immense blessings I have had, the longings of my heart accomplished."

On August 13, 1910, Florence Nightingale fell asleep at noon and did not wake again. She had lived ninety years and three months.

In accordance with her wishes, she was buried in the churchyard at East Wellow, near Embley, beside her father and mother. There is only the simplest of inscriptions on the fourth side of the family tombstone: *F.N. born 1820. Died 1910.*

The Lamp Burns On

FLORENCE NIGHTINGALE is remembered chiefly for the two years she spent in the Crimea—a short time in her long and productive life. But those were critical years, for it was during the ordeal in Crimea that she was first able to test her ideas on trained nursing. And it was through her work in the Crimea that she won the fame which made her later work possible.

All soldiers owe a debt of gratitude to Florence Nightingale. For it was she who started the far-reaching reforms that affect their health and well-being today.

The International Red Cross grew out of the inspiration she gave to a Swiss gentleman, Henri Dunant. He said it was her work in the Crimea which inspired him to start the Red Cross movement.

District Nursing, for the care of the sick and poor in their own homes, was also inspired by Florence Nightingale. In the United States this vital service is performed by the Visiting Nurses organization.

But her greatest contribution was in the field of hospital nursing, with the career opportunities it has opened for women.

Florence Nightingale did not, of course, *originate* nursing.

What she did was found *modern nursing,* with its use of special training and knowledge. Because of her special knowledge and dedication, what she demonstrated was nursing as an art and a respected profession.

The influence of the Nightingale Training School was worldwide. Several such nursing schools were soon established throughout the United States. In 1889 Miss Louisa Parsons, a much-honored graduate of the Nightingale School, came to the United States as a superintendent of the new training school for nurses in the University of Maryland Hospital in Baltimore. Miss Parsons arrived with a new uniform for nurses, designed by Miss Nightingale. This was a gray-and-white-striped cotton dress, white apron with a square bib, black stockings, and black high-topped shoes. She also brought with her the gift of a lovely fluted lace cap to be awarded to the students when they finished their probation period. Thus the Maryland School of Nursing inherited the Nightingale cap, an honor of which its nurses are still very proud.

By 1910 there were more than one thousand training schools for nurses in the United States alone. All were the outgrowth of Florence Nightingale's work. In May of that year, a huge meeting was held in New York City to honor the fiftieth anniversary of the first Nightingale Training School in London, and "to testify to the admiration of the entire American people for Florence Nightingale's great record and noble life."

The Nightingale School in London is still part of St. Thomas's Hospital. It now graduates about 120 "Nightingales" a year. It still remains true in spirit to the intentions of its founder. The professional qualities and the bedside skills which Florence Nightingale required of her nurses are in even greater demand today than they were in her lifetime.

Florence Nightingale made of nursing a noble profession, and stamped her own image on it. "Nursing is an art," she said, "and if it is to be made an art, it requires as exclusive a devotion, as hard preparation, as any painter's or sculptor's work; for what is having to do with dead canvas or cold marble compared with having to do with the living body—the temple of God's spirit."

Florence Nightingale's lamp burns as bright as ever, as thousands of young nurses symbolically light their candles at their graduation ceremonies. All nurses, when they graduate, also recite a solemn pledge. Many of them believe that they are speaking Florence Nightingale's own words. But Florence never exacted any vows from her nurses. This pledge reflects not her words but her ideals for the nursing profession. And, although it was composed in the United States, the pledge has linked nurses the world over, for it has been translated into many languages. Nurses today would feel "ungraduated" if the Nightingale pledge were to be left out of their closing ceremonies.

Florence Nightingale, who wanted no monuments, lives in these words:

I solemnly pledge myself before God and in the presence of this assembly, to pass my life in purity and to practice my profession faithfully. I will abstain from whatever is deleterious and mischievous, and will not take or knowingly administer any harmful drug. I will do all in my power to maintain and elevate the standard of my profession, and will hold in confidence all personal matters committed to my keeping and all family affairs coming to my knowledge in the practice of my calling. With loyalty will I endeavor to aid the physician in his work, and devote myself to the welfare of those committed to my care.

With every candle lit for the graduating ceremony, Florence Nightingale's lamp glows brighter.

The Nightingale pledge was drawn
up at the old Harper Hospital in
Detroit, Michigan, and was
first used by its graduating class in the spring
of 1893. Fittingly, it
is an adaptation of
the Hippocratic
oath taken by
physicians.

DATES AND EVENTS IN
THE LIFE OF FLORENCE NIGHTINGALE

1820   May 12, Florence Nightingale born in Florence, Italy.

1837   February 7, Florence receives what she believes to be a call from God to His service.

1839   May 24, Florence and her sister Parthe are presented to Victoria on the young queen's twentieth birthday.

1842   May, Florence meets Richard Monckton Milnes.
Florence realizes that her life work lies among the poor; that she must work in the hospitals.

1845   Florence tries to go to the Salisbury Infirmary to train as a nurse, but is prevented by her horrified family.

1847–48   Florence spends the winter in Rome with the Bracebridges; visits hospitals, orphanages; studies the work of the Catholic sisters in these institutions.

1849   Florence refuses Richard Milnes's proposal of marriage.

1850   July 31, through the kindness and understanding of Selina Bracebridge, Florence is able to visit Kaiserswerth for two weeks.

1851   July to October, Florence goes to Kaiserswerth for nearly four months.

1852   Florence nurses her father when his eyesight is threatened. Mr. Nightingale settles a comfortable sum of money on his daughter, allowing her to live independently, if she wishes.

1853   August 12, Florence becomes Superintendent of the Institution for the Care of Sick Gentlewomen in Distressed Circumstances.

1854   March, Britain declares war on Russia (the Crimean War).
       August, Florence nurses cholera cases at the Middlesex
       Hospital in London.
       October 19, Florence Nightingale is appointed Superin-
       tendent of the Female Nursing Establishment of the
       English General Hospitals in Turkey.
       October 21, Florence and her nurses leave London for
       Scutari, arriving at the Barrack Hospital on November 4.

1855   May 5, Florence visits the fighting front in the Crimea.
       Contracts "Crimean fever" and is near death. Declared
       out of danger May 24, she returns to Scutari.
       September 8, Sevastopol falls to the British, ending the
       Crimean War, though the peace treaty is not signed until
       March 30, 1856.

1856   August 7, Florence returns to her family's home in Eng-
       land.

1858   Florence's *Notes on the Army* and the report of the royal
       commission on army health reforms are published.

1859   Florence Nightingale's book *Notes on Hospitals* is pub-
       lished. She becomes world authority on the subject.
       December, *Notes on Nursing* is published and becomes
       an immediate popular success.

1860   July 9, Nightingale Training School is opened at St.
       Thomas's Hospital in London.

1861   October, Florence is asked by President Lincoln's Secre-
       tary of War for help in organizing soldiers' hospitals during
       the Civil War in the United States.

1897   Diamond jubilee of Queen Victoria; exhibition of the pro-
       gress in nursing during the Victorian era, planned around
       the pioneer work of Florence Nightingale.

1907   June, Florence is honored by the Red Cross Congress in
       London.
       December, she is awarded the Order of Merit.

1910   August 13, Florence Nightingale dies in her sleep at the
       age of ninety years and three months.

FOR FURTHER READING

Notes on Nursing: What It Is, and What It Is Not, by Florence Nightingale (D. Appleton & Co., 1926; originally published in 1859). Charming, wise and warm; as fresh today as the day it was written. Replica edition 1957, J. B. Lippincott Co.

The Life of Florence Nightingale, by Sir Edward Cook (The Macmillan Company, London and New York, 1913, 1942). The official, definitive biography.

Florence Nightingale, by Cecil Woodham-Smith (McGraw-Hill Book Co., Inc., 1951). Excellent, definitive, utilizes papers not available to Sir Edward.

Lonely Crusader, by Cecil Woodham-Smith (Whittlesey House, 1951). Condensed, young adult version of the above.

A Lost Commander: Florence Nightingale, by Mary Shipman Andrews (Doubleday, Doran, 1929).

Eminent Victorians, by Lytton Strachey (G. P. Putnam's Sons, Capricorn Books, 1963; originally published 1918). Short account in a group of biographies.

Florence Nightingale, by Lucy Ridgely Seymer (The Macmillan Company, London and New York, 1950). The author is a Nightingale Nurse, a graduate of the Nightingale Training School at St. Thomas's Hospital in London.

Florence Nightingale 1820–1856, by Ida B. O'Malley (Butterworth & Co., London, 1931). The author drew on personal notes, letters, journals—and in particular on a series of copybooks, written in French by Florence at the age of eight or nine to please a favorite governess, and titled *La Vie de Florence Rossignol.*

The Young Florence Nightingale, by Lettice U. Cooper (Roy Publishers, 1960). Also based on the above copybooks.

Florence Nightingale's Nuns, by Emmeline Garnett (Farrar, Straus & Cudahy, 1961). A different point of view.

Florence Nightingale, by Laura E. Richards (D. Appleton & Co., 1909). The author drew on the *Reminiscences* of her mother, Julia Ward Howe.

A History of the Nursing Profession, by Brian Abel-Smith (Heinemann, London, 1960).

The Story of Nursing, by Bertha S. Dodge (Little, Brown and Co., 1954).

The First Woman Doctor: The Story of Elizabeth Blackwell, M.D., by Rachel Baker (Julian Messner, Inc., 1944).

ABOUT THE AUTHOR AND THE ILLUSTRATOR

LEE WYNDHAM was born in Russia, and as a young girl she spent three years within sight of Scutari, where Florence Nightingale nursed the victims of the Crimean War. She lived directly across the Bosporus, on one of the green hills above Constantinople, recuperating in a sanitarium from a series of illnesses contracted after her family's escape from Russia at the time of the revolution. "My father was a White Russian officer in the Tsar's army," she says, "and I have been in Sevastopol, in the Crimea, with a retreating army. There are many scenes of war imprinted on my mind, and I know that I saw many of the sights Florence Nightingale saw, and heard many of the sounds she heard. I felt, in writing this book, that I could enter into her life and time, and hopefully bring her to life for my young readers."

Mrs. Wyndham is married to Robert Wyndham, who is, like her, a writer, lecturer, and editor. Together they write a syndicated review column, The Junior Book Shelf. The author of more than forty published books, Mrs. Wyndham has inspired the writing of many more, through the course in writing children's books that she teaches at New York University's Writing Center. Mr. and Mrs. Wyndham have a grown son and a daughter, and live in Morristown, New Jersey.

RICHARD CUFFARI, a graduate of Pratt Institute, is a children's book illustrator and a painter. He has exhibited in New York galleries and has been represented in AIGA design shows and in those of the Society of Illustrators. A resident of Brooklyn, he is married and has four children.

1   2   3   4   5   73   72   70   71   69